395

Granada
and
Eastern Andalucia

Granada

Granada
and
Eastern Andalucia

David Hewson

MEREHURST PRESS
LONDON

Published 1990 by Merehurst Press
Ferry House, 51-7 Lacy Road
Putney, London SW15 1PR

© Merehurst Ltd 1990

ISBN 1 85391 037 6

Designed and produced by Snap! Books
Typeset by David Hewson and Lin-Art, Ashford,
Kent, UK
Illustrations by Ann Johns.
Cover illustration: Hansen, 'A View of Granada,'
reproduced by kind permission of Christie's,
London/The Bridgeman Art Library, London

Maps by Sue Lawes
Printed in Great Britain by Butler and Tanner,
Frome, Somerset

Contents

Granada

Author's Preface

This is designed to be a practical guide to a part of Spain which has much to offer the independent traveller. Practicality can be a rarity in travel books. Many assume that the modern visitor is still on the Grand Tour, unconfined by time or expense in his explorations, and meticulously describe a region in such detail that one scours the map to find a way of including everything in the itinerary. Or they follow the other school and regard southern Spain as little but a holiday playground, and excursions to great cities like Granada as fantasy days out in some great theme park.

Yet Andalucia is a wonderful area for anyone whose interests fall somewhere between these two; those of us who are fascinated by a vibrant and exotic culture but also want our share of regional food and wine, a decent bed for the night, and as much to see as is practically possible in the time to spare. So you will find here a *selective* guide to what you might reasonably hope to do in the space of two weeks in this lovely corner of Spain, with recommendations for hotels and restaurants to meet a range of budgets.

It is this search for practicality which has led me to divide Andalucia into two parts for the purpose of this series, with the companion volume *Seville and Western Andalucia*. The greatest mistake the new visitor to Andalucia can make is to try to see everything in one fell swoop, often through a frantic circular journey taking in Granada, Córdoba, Seville and Ronda. At the close, the poor souls wilt into Málaga airport for their homeward flight, their minds swimming with a jumble of images as Granada's Alhambra blends mystically with the Giralda tower of Seville and the forest of columns in Córdoba's Mezquita. It is impossible to make this particular journey without gaining the distinct, and wholly inaccurate, impression that Andalucia is clogged to the gills with tourists of all shapes and sizes and that there is scarcely a green leaf in the place, save those carefully tended ones which flourish in the Generalife gardens.

One cannot travel the whole of Andalucia in less than a month, and even then great sights will still be left out. If you have the time, then these two titles will enable you to describe a double eight through the region discovering many parts the whistlestop tourist will never see. This volume deals with eastern Andalucia where the traveller will find the Alhambra of Granada, the peaceful Alpujarra and the majestic Cazorla mountain ranges, those two delightful twin Renaissance towns of Ubeda and Baeza, and the curious cave dwellers of Guadix.

The journey begins at the regional capital of Málaga and, in the space of 12 nights, travels inland to the cities of Granada and Córdoba, north east to Ubeda, on the very edge of Andalucia, then south through Cazorla to Guadix. A mountain pass leads into the remote Alpujarra range and on to the Mediterranean coast near Almuñécar where the main road leads back to Málaga.

These are visits which may be made quite casually for most of the year. Having booked the first few nights of your journey, you may continue to book ahead as you travel, and the itinerary outlined here is one which can be tailored to individual tastes and requirements. Only at the popular state hotels, the paradors, does advance booking become essential all year round, and these are clearly marked. Each day is prefaced by a summary of the journey ahead, followed by route details, places of interest, and finally advice on the best hotels and restaurants in the area.

It took me several attempts to learn to approach Spain at the measured pace which the country demands, and it is the lessons from my mistakes which I hope to pass on to the reader. I have been fortunate enough to be helped in this enterprise by the many Spanish people I encountered on my travels who were only too keen to assist me. My friend José, of the Doña Lupe Hotel in Granada, was a source of sound advice and encouragement throughout, and without him this would be a poorer book.

Introduction
to
Eastern Andalucia

La Calahorra

The exotic character of Andalucia has entranced visitors for centuries. Fine buildings, lively cities, and superb, unspoilt countryside typify a region which gave birth to Bizet's *Carmen* and the *Tales of the Alhambra* of the 19th-century American writer Washington Irving. The modernisation of Spain has given Andalucia many comfortable hotels, good roads for the independent traveller, and an abundance of fine food and wine from throughout the Iberian peninsula.

It is the culture of the region which sets Andalucia apart from the rest of Europe. It is a land with a different past, one rooted as much in the ways of Islam as it is in Christianity. There are obvious and beautiful legacies, such as Granada's Alhambra and Córdoba's mosque, the Mezquita. There are also less visible signs rooted in the character of the people themselves and the customs and traditions they so assiduously maintain. These are people who inhabit a flamboyant and convivial part of Europe, who are fond of song and dance and the chatter of human voices in tiled patios. Piety and sensuality stand side by side with no apparent contradiction. The ties of family and church remain largely intact in the face of the modernisations sweeping Spain since it emerged from the dark years of Franco. It is a culture which has proved as durable as it is exciting, and one feels very lucky to be able to witness it so close to home.

History

Southern Spain has been populated by man since the stone age. Greek settlers and later Carthaginians made the land part of their Mediterranean territory which the Romans later took into their empire, controlling the whole of the peninsula by 206 BC. The provincial capital was established at Córdoba. The collapse of the Roman empire led to invasion by Vandals from the north in the fifth century AD and it was they who gave the region its modern name – Andalucia being a corruption of the Arabic *Al-Andalus*, land of the Vandals. Their tenure was brief. They were expelled by Visigoths who ruled Spain as Christians from the fifth century to the beginning of the eighth when Arab forces from North Africa crossed the Straits of Gibraltar and, within three years, conquered the whole of Iberia.

11

In 756, the Arab prince Abderrahman left Damascus, which was torn by feuding factions, landing at Almuñécar to declare Al-Andalus an independent emirate, and beginning the process of turning Córdoba into its capital. Córdoba of the ninth and tenth centuries was a city famed throughout Europe for its beauty, wealth and learning. His dynasty, the Ommiads, lasted until the beginning of the 11th century when dissent among the ruling families led to the break-up of the state into independent kingdoms known as Taifas, each ruled by an individual head of state. This was a move which was to hasten the end of Moslem Spain, for these small kingdoms were in no position to resist the growing power of the united Christian states in the north determined to reconquer the peninsula. Many Moslem rulers made pacts with the Christians to support campaigns against their fellow Islamic caliphs; the tide had turned.

North African Arabs, the Almoravids and the Almohads, took control of parts of Al-Andalus but they could not prevent the fall of its two most important cities, Córdoba and Seville, in 1236 and 1248 respectively. Al-Andalus had disappeared apart from the kingdom of Granada which had been on the Christian side in the fall of Seville. It was this precarious existence which turned the Nazari dynasty of Granada into the pleasure-loving aesthetes who created the Alhambra. Their guarantees of independence were to mean nothing to the ambitious Christian monarchs Ferdinand and Isabel who, in 1492, forced the abdication of the king Boabdil and united Spain under Christianity for the first time in nearly eight centuries.

It will be seen from this all-too-brief history that there is no easy way to describe the Moslem rulers of Al-Andalus. Some were North African and generally referred to as 'Moors', some were light-skinned Arabs from the east. The average citizen of the state from the tenth century onwards probably looked much like the average Andalucian resident of today. For this reason, I have referred throughout to Moslem culture, not that of the Arabs or the Moors, though you will see the latter term used frequently to describe artefacts which have no connection with North Africa whatsoever.

The Moslem period left Andalucia with a gorgeous legacy of architecture and culture which continues to shape the region's character today. It was the zenith of the region's artistic life, against which even the Renaissance charm of towns like Ubeda and Baeza must pale. After the Reconquest, eastern Andalucia saw its importance to the newly united Christian kingdom diminish as Spain began to look to the New World. The Western cities of Seville and Cádiz grew rich on trade with the New World, leaving their eastern cousins in the shade. To this day there remains between Seville and Granada a degree of rivalry which occasionally borders on hostility.

Eastern Andalucia was little more than a spectator in the chaotic disintegration of the Spanish state which began with the defeat of the Armada in 1588. Both Córdoba and Granada declined in importance and in economic stature. By the early 19th century, the Alhambra itself, once the symbol of Moslem greatness in Spain, was largely a ruin. During the Spanish Civil War, Nationalists rapidly took hold of the south of the country, with Seville as their headquarters. In 1936, the Granadino poet Federico Garcia Lorca was murdered by Nationalist thugs, the best known of many victims of this bloody episode in Spain's history.

In the early 1960s, the Costa del Sol saw the birth of the package holiday boom which was to lead to an economic transformation of the coast which simultaneously enriched many of the local inhabitants while destroying much of the shoreline. Small fishing villages like Torremolinos and Marbella became, in the space of a few years, large, modern tourist resorts which, in parts, manage to retain some flavour of Spain. Only a few miles beyond the resort belt, however, Andalucia is little changed, a largely agricultural society which has prospered in recent years.

Geography

Andalucia is one of Spain's seventeen autonomous regions, covering 34,700 square miles from the Atlantic to the Mediterranean. The eastern section covered in this book is dominated by the mountain range of the Sierra Nevada which has permanent snow on its highest peaks. The journey passes through four very different provinces – coastal Málaga, with a mild climate caused by its position at the foot of the sierra, Granada, which consists both of the fertile plain, the *vega*, and the mountains extending south through the Alpujarra to the coast, Córdoba, lying in the hot Guadalquivir basin, and Jaen, an olive growing region with the high, humid mountains of the Sierra de Cazorla range to the east.

The principal river of the area is the Guadalquivir, which rises in the Sierra de Cazorla and flows, through Córdoba on to Seville and the Atlantic in western Andalucia.

The traditional crops of the region are olives and grapes. Sugar cane was introduced to the coast around Motril more than two centuries ago and still supports a small rum distilling industry. In recent years, European tastes for exotic fruit and vegetables have led to experiments in farming techniques around the coast. Avocado farms and specialist growers of exotic fruits, such as the kiwi fruit and chirimoya, are common. There are wide regional variations in weather, from the typical Mediterranean climate of Málaga to Jaen's cold winters and boiling summers.

Art and Architecture

The climate of southern Spain has long attracted artists, both native and foreign. Picasso was born in Málaga and owed much to a flourishing modernist school of art which existed in the city as he grew up. Granada was the home of the great composer Manuel de Falla. Both reflected the vivid and unique Mediterranean culture of Andalucia and remain much loved today. Among modern foreign writers, Laurie Lee, whose travels in the 1930s are marked by a statue on the seafront in Almuñécar, and Gerald Brenan, who documented life in the Alpujarra, stand out for a particular sympathy with the people of southern Spain.

Churches and galleries throughout the region bear witness to the golden age of Andalucian art, in the 17th century, when the Sevillian School was at its best. Alonso Cano, a Granadino sculptor and painter, came to rank alongside the greatest of the Sevillian artists, such as Murillo, and is represented in several places visited on this itinerary. Fine carving and wrought ironwork also typify the church art of Andalucia. The early 20th-century painter Julio Romero de Torres of Córdoba is not a household name outside Spain, but his work has adorned many a British and American domestic wall. Torres was the creator of a generation of dusky-skinned Spanish beauties whose sultry poses captured a little of the essence of Andalucia while at the same time outraging the city's church elders.

Architecture is dominated by the influence of the Moslem occupation. Elements of the Alhambra and other great Arab buildings are copied and made commonplace on everyday buildings. The makers of construction materials still produce tiles, arches, columns and other architectural effects which are copied from originals seen in Moslem architecture dating from the 12th century and earlier, and very popular they remain too, though it is a little strange to see a classical horseshoe arch adorning the outside of a modern garage.

After the Reconquest, Christian architects set out to prove their cultural superiority in a blaze of rather heavy-handed cathedrals and secular buildings which, in the main, are frankly rather ugly. Only in the delightful Renaissance towns of Baeza and Ubeda does one begin to grasp the architectural delicacy and charm which some craftsmen of the 16th and 17th centuries could achieve.

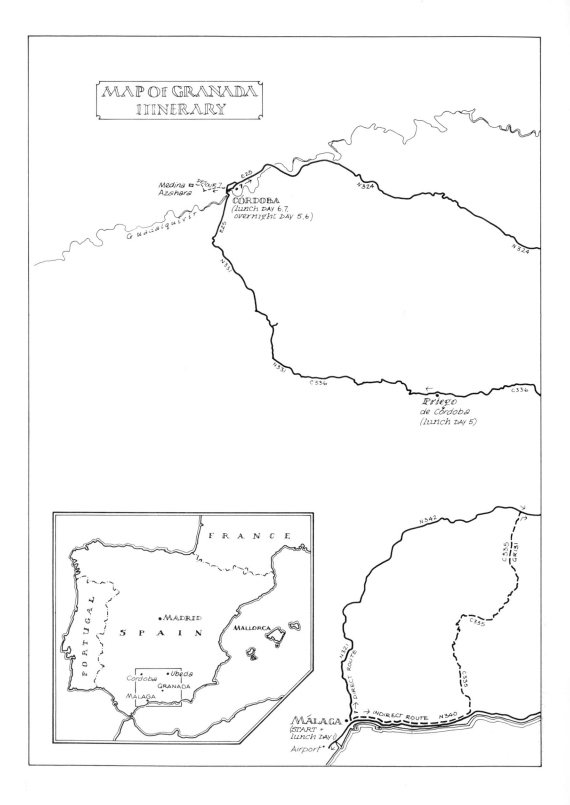

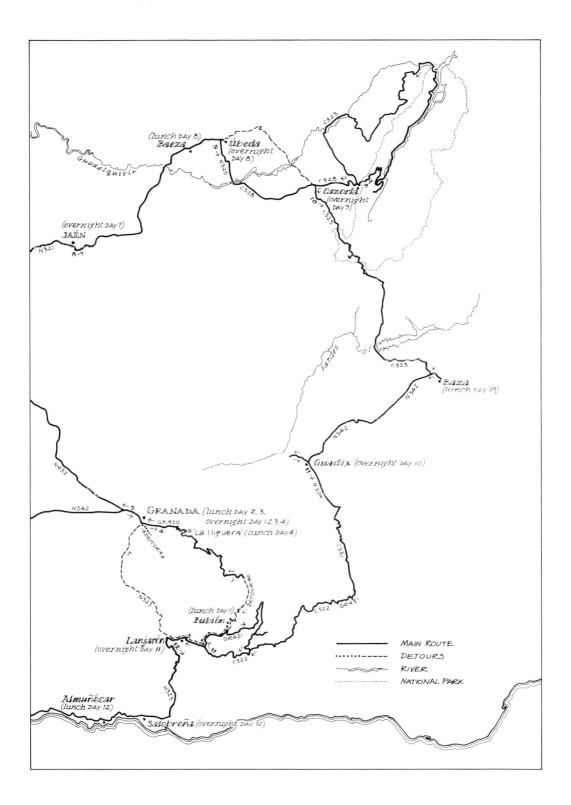

Baeza

The Epicure's Guide

Food

Andalucia is a lush and abundant land. The coast east of Nerja is now one of the largest producers of specialist fruit and vegetables in Europe, growing vast fields of avocados, kumquats, medlars, melons and sugar cane. The vega around Granada is rich in citrus fruit and kitchen vegetables, while one need only venture into the main market of Málaga to see how abundant the seas of the Mediterranean remain, in spite of blatant overfishing in parts. In the hills of the Alpujarra, small farmers cure *jamón serrano*, mountain ham, in the clear air to produce a delicacy renowned throughout Spain.

But this cornucopia would mean nothing without a culinary tradition to exploit it. The kitchens of Andalucia combine several different traditions, each based on the best of the local produce available in the markets. At the coast this centres, naturally, around fresh fish and seafood, served plainly, fried to a dry perfection or, in the case of shellfish, *a la plancha*, grilled with garlic and a few herbs.

Inland, one soon encounters the hearty meals of the mountains, based on pork, eggs, and a marvellous accompaniment called *migas*, made from stale breadcrumbs fried in olive oil with peppers and garlic. In Córdoba, there is a purposeful determination to resurrect the traditions of Moslem days in the synthesis called Mozarabic cuisine, in which meat and fowl are often cooked with fruit, sugar and honey. And in the north, around Ubeda and Cazorla, there is a more temperate feel to the kitchens. The seasonings are less exotic, the food plainer, with wild goat and boar appearing frequently, and at very reasonable prices.

These regional variations can be so great that I have prefaced the restaurant guide for each part of this journey with a brief description of local specialities wherever applicable. There are, however, two Andalucian staple dishes which one will see almost everywhere: *gazpacho*, the refreshing cold soup based on tomatoes, and *paella*. Gazpacho is such an easy dish to make that one will rarely encounter a poor example. The sign of an authentic restaurant is when the soup is served with extra garnishes, usually chopped tomatoes, cucumber and onions. It is a simple dish, perfect for a boiling summer day and composed entirely of raw local ingredients.

Paella is a different matter altogether, and may vary enormously in quality throughout the region. The dish is originally from Valencia, the rice growing region of Spain, where it is often made with rabbit. The Andalucian version demands fish, shellfish and chicken and, of course, saffron. True paella will be expensive and cooked to order for a minimum of two people. The best on this journey will be served in Málaga.

One cannot talk about Spanish food without mentioning *tapas*, the small platefuls available in bars. For the hungry Spaniard, tapas may be simply a snack before he goes out for an evening meal. Those of us with more moderate appetites can happily spend the night wandering from bar to bar trying a selection of these little dishes, which may include a piece of fried fish, a few mussels, octopus, local sausage or a few slivers of ham. Most of the towns on this journey are sufficiently unspoilt by tourism not to have lost the old habit of handing out a small plate of tapas for free whenever the customer buys a glass of wine or a beer (but not with any other drink). Beyond this gift, one will usually be able to inspect a *carta* of tapas or a board behind the bar on which prices are marked. These will normally be divided into two columns – one for the tapa or small plate, and a second for the *ración*, a larger portion normally bought to share between a group of people.

I have recommended a few tapas establishments in the pages that follow, but I am unwilling to guide the traveller too much. Part of the pleasure of a journey lies in following one's nose through the local streets of Spain and discovering what surprises lurk around the corner.

The Spanish are trenchermen – and women – at the table, eating long and hard, preferably into the early hours. Breakfast is usually a cup of coffee and a cake or *churro*, the latter being a curl of doughnut freshly fried and dunked into the coffee cup. A mid-morning tapas of cheese or the ever present sandwich of cheese, ham or even squid is common. Lunch is taken late, with many restaurants not opening their doors until 1.30pm, and will often run to two or three courses.

The main meal of the day is dinner, which is rarely begun before 9.30, though the hungry may often stoke up on a few courses of tapas before finally settling on a restaurant for the evening. The speed with which Spanish restaurants become full can be disconcerting. A recommended place which seems empty and on the verge of bankruptcy at 8.45pm may well be bursting to the gills an hour later. Do regard reservations as essential for the more expensive restaurants recommended here.

Wine and Other Drinks

There are no great table wines made in the south of Spain. The climate is too fierce to produce noteworthy vintages to excite the wine writers of national newspapers. For great wine, one turns to the well-known region of Rioja, north of Madrid, with its heavy oaky reds and whites. You will find them stocked everywhere, popular and reliable brands being Paternina, Marqués de Caceres, Torres and Réné Barbier.

Spanish rosés, *rosados*, are greatly neglected by the foreign visitor. The best, inevitably, are from Rioja though you will also find palatable offerings from lesser-known regions such as Peñedes, more reminiscent of a good flinty Tavel than the Mateus of neighbouring Portugal, and make for a pleasant compromise between a heavy red or a white. Red table wines are frequently served chilled in summer. The most popular light white wine is Monopole, although I find it rather characterless. A new generation of white Riojas which have not been subjected to oak is now appearing, led by the Marqués de Caceres brand. To the average Andalucian, however, white wine means either sherry, *jerez*, or the similar *montilla*, both of which are drunk freely at all times of the day. The true native of eastern Andalucia will always prefer montilla, which comes from the town of the same name south of Córdoba, over sherry, which is a product of the west and the many bodegas around the town of Jerez.

The Spanish possess the customary Mediterranean facility to make spirits from the most curious of sources. Artichokes, mountain herbs and pomegranates form the basis of several liqueurs which stand largely undrunk on the shelves of many cafés.

The most popular spirit is brandy, which is available in many different degrees of sophistication, from the roughest to brands which stand comparison with good French cognac. The better class brandies of the great sherry houses, such as Terry, Osborne and Domecq, are reliable, and Osborne's curiously named Soberano line can be relied upon to satisfy the sceptical cognac lover, even if it studiously fails to live up to its name when taken in quantity. Rum, from the distilleries of Motril and Salobreña, is another powerful spirit, though one declining in popularity as the drinkers of Spain look for more international cocktails. Whisky and gin, imported and copied locally, are extremely popular, and there are several versions of anis which make a passable Pernod.

The sweetness of the Spanish palate is reflected in the dessert wine called, simply, *Málaga* which has waned in popularity in recent years. I suspect it is due for a measure of rediscovery, given the new liking for treacly 'pudding wines' such as Beaumes de Venise. Another Spanish dessert wine well worth sampling, though it is not local to Andalucia, is the Moscatel of Valencia.

The commonest long drink is beer, inevitably the fizzy, golden lager of the Mediterranean. The *tinto de verano*, literally 'summer red', is popular on a hot day and consists of a splash of red wine with Casera, a soft drink like Seven Up, or soda water. The only unique soft drink worth recording in Andalucia is the curious *horchata*, a milky concoction made from crushed tiny artichokes sometimes known as tiger nuts. It is a little sweet but more refreshing than the average Spanish beer and originated in Valencia.

Coffee is strong and normally served *solo*, that is black, in a small cup, like Italian espresso. A large black coffee is 'uno solo grande'. Coffee with milk, *cafe con leche*, is simply solo with hot milk added, though Italian capuchinos are occasionally offered. Instant coffee, invariably christened 'Nescafé' whatever the brand, is usually available. Tea is most often served with lemon, *con limón*, and there is a common herb tea, *manzanilla*, which, confusingly, is also the name of a very dry and excellent sherry.

Handy Tips

HOW TO GET THERE FROM THE UK
The itinerary begins at Málaga. I suggest you arrive there the night before
setting out on the route.

By Air — There is no easier destination in Spain from the UK than Málaga.
Each day throughout the year there are plenty of scheduled and chartered
carriers heading for the Costa del Sol. Cheap charter tickets are available
throughout the year.

By Car — The fastest route recommended by the AA is to enter Spain by
San Sebastián and travel to Seville via Burgos, and Madrid, then taking the
fast NIV to Seville via Valdepeñas and Córdoba. The AA will produce for
members excellent individual itineraries, outlining routes to Spain from
the Channel ports which take into account roadworks, if contacted at least
two weeks before departure. In general, the recommended route south
from Calais and Boulogne skirts Paris on the Boulevard Périphérique, leaving by the A10 south through Tours and Bordeaux. It is advisable to check
on roadworks and other possible delays in advance. Spain is currently suf-
fering a rash of thefts from cars. Wherever possible park in a secure garage
in large cities, and never leave possessions in view.

WHEN TO GO
The most pleasant time to visit Andalucia is in May or early June,
September or early October. The temperatures are moderate and sun is
virtually guaranteed. Winters are normally mild and relatively dry,
although Granada, situated near the mountains of the Sierra Nevada, can
be chilly and wet. The consolation for the winter visitor is that there are
also times when the weather is beautiful and the main sights are always less
crowded. In the height of summer, the coast and Granada are cooled by
pleasant breezes but many inland places suffer from the heat.

FESTIVALS AND OTHER EVENTS

Spain is a land of fairs, processions and festivals. Many have religious origins but are now simply enormous social gatherings at which one may see dancing, music, showmen and stall after stall of food and drink. The Spanish do not retire early at the best of times, and during festivals will happily stay up all night long, chattering and dancing into the early hours. Bear this in mind when booking a hotel during festival time.

Semana Santa is the most spectacular of all festivals and takes place each Easter. That of Seville is best known, but the celebrations in Granada and Málaga are almost as colourful. Holy Week is a time of intense piety, vivid parades, singing and flamenco.

The Albaicín district of Granada celebrates the Cruces de Mayo at the beginning of May when streets and squares are decorated with flowers in a celebration which has pagan origins. At the end of May, Córdoba celebrates its popular Feria de Mayo, two weeks of dancing and music which occupy virtually the whole of the Av. Argentina. Nerja holds a traditional pilgrimage, the Romeria, on May 15. Corpus Christi is a similar celebration in Granada at the beginning of June. In the same month, Trevélez (p. 123) holds its 'Moors and Christians' celebrations, and the village also has a pilgrimage to the summit of Mulhacén on August 5. The biggest international cultural event of the area is the open air classical music festival held in the Generalife in June and July.

PUBLIC HOLIDAYS

There are fixed national public holidays on January 1 and 6; May 1; July 25; August 15; November 1; December 6, 8 and 25. The week before Easter is a national holiday for Holy Week, during which many businesses close or operate a restricted service. In addition to these national holidays most towns and villages observe local saints' days.

BANKS

Banks are open from 9am until 2am on weekdays and 9am to 1pm on Saturdays. Eurocheques, backed by a guarantee card, are commonly accepted in hotels, restaurants and shops. Many UK cashcards can now be used in 24-hour Spanish cash dispenser machines though prior arrangements may need to be made with the user's bank.

SHOPPING
The majority of shops creak into life around 9.30am and shut again between 1pm and 2pm, reopening between 4.30pm and about 8pm. In resort areas a number of shops now stay open all day, as does the large El Corte Inglés in Málaga.

MONUMENTS AND MUSEUMS
The normal opening hours are from 10am to 1.30pm and 4.30pm to 6.30pm. Some extend the closing time in the evening until 8pm. Only the Alhambra remains open all day.

DRIVING
The speed limits are: 60km/h (37mph) in built-up areas, 100km/h (62mph) on main roads, 120km/h (74mph) on motorways, and 90km/h (56mph) on other roads.

The main Málaga-Cádiz highway is one of the most notorious in Europe, hence its nickname of *La Carretera del Muerte*, the highway of death. There are two common causes of accidents: pedestrians trying to dash across the road, and cars trying to make an unauthorised left turn. *Always* use the slip roads built to allow left turns to be made more safely through turning right and then across the road.

Car hire from the large international companies tends to be around 30 per cent more expensive than that offered by domestic car hire firms unless pre-booked through special offers. It is easy to pick up a hire car at Málaga airport without pre-booking if you must. Pre-booking is advisable to guarantee the price paid for a vehicle. The Spanish car hire industry has many little tricks designed to extract extra pesetas from the unwary. Always ensure that the price paid for a pre-booked car includes all taxes, collision damage waiver, and delivery charges. If this is not possible, ascertain in advance what extras you will have to pay at the airport.

Most companies charge an additional fee for delivering cars outside normal office hours and at weekends. It is also customary to take a deposit for the petrol already in the car, though the representatives of some companies are difficult to track down when the time comes to reclaim your deposit. There is no substitute for an advance car hire receipt which stipulates that all parts of the hire have been pre-paid.

LANGUAGE

Andalucians speak Castilian – that is, 'normal' Spanish – with a local accent. The most noticeable regional characteristic is to pronounce 'c' as a soft 's' instead of 'th': in other words *gracias* is pronounced 'grasias' not 'grathias' as it is elsewhere in Spain.

KEY TO ITINERARY

Ratings are an indication of the cost of a room or meal, not a judgement on the quality of the establishment, all of which are good within their price range.

**	Reasonable	****	Expensive
***	Average	*****	Very expensive

To follow the Itinerary I recommend you use Michelin Map Spanish series no. 446. Within the text there is a general map of the area on p. 16, and detailed routes as follows:

Days 1-4, p. 30   Days 9-10, p.110
Days 5-8, p. 90   Days 11-12, p.131

At the beginning of each day in the Itinerary there is a summary of the day's route and grid references of the places visited. Grid references are latitude first, then longitude (i.e. reading from the perimeter of the map, the vertical number then the horizontal). Each square represents 20'.

The Itinerary

DAY 1

Málaga to Granada by Alhama de Granada, around 100 miles.

The itinerary begins with a visit to Málaga, the busy city which is the capital of the Costa del Sol. The hilltop parador provides spectacular views across the bay and a pleasant walk, through ancient fortifications, into the city. The Cathedral, the Museo de Bellas Artes, and the main market, on the site of an Arabic shipyard, are the principal sights. Local restaurants are famous for their seafood. A scenic route from Málaga leads to the town of Alhama de Granada, set on the edge of a gorge, and the journey continues through the vega on to Granada.

Overnight in Granada.

Map references
Málaga	36 42´N 4 25´W
Loja	37 10´N 4 08´W
Vélez Málaga	36 44´N 4 05´W
Alhama de Granada	37 02´N 3 59´W
Santafé	37 15´N 3 45´W
Granada	37 10´N 3 35´W

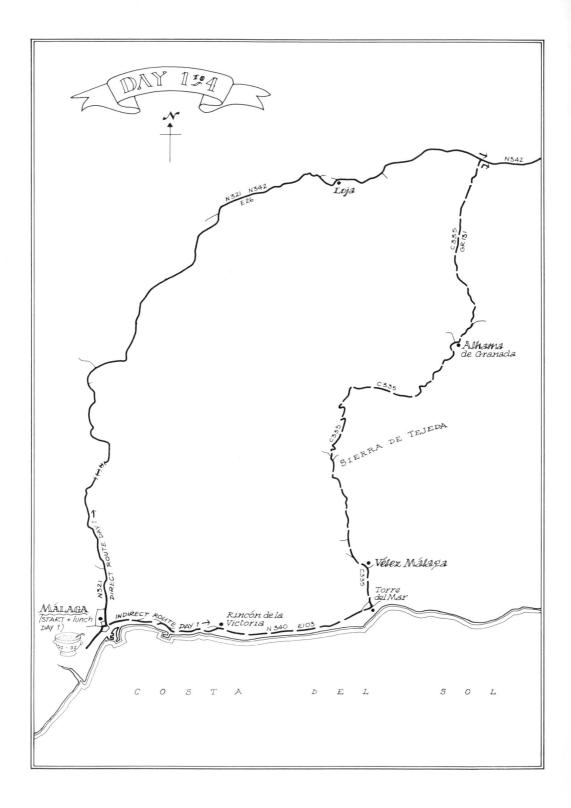

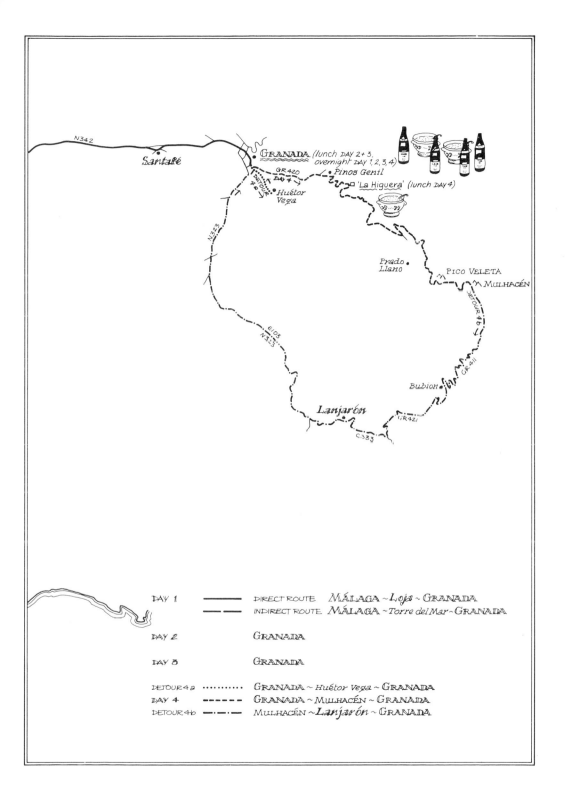

N342

Santafé

GRANADA *(lunch DAY 2 + 3, overnight DAY 1, 2, 3, 4)*

GR 420
DAY 1
DETOUR 4a
Pinos Genil

'La Higuera' *(lunch DAY 4)*

Huétor Vega

N323

Prado Llano

PICO VELETA
MULHACÉN

DETOUR 4b

GR 411

GR 103
N333

Bubion

GR 421

Lanjarón

C.333

DAY 1 ——————— DIRECT ROUTE   MÁLAGA ~ *Loja* ~ GRANADA
        — — — — — INDIRECT ROUTE MÁLAGA ~ *Torre del Mar* ~ GRANADA

DAY 2   GRANADA

DAY 3   GRANADA

DETOUR 4a ·············   GRANADA ~ *Huétor Vega* ~ GRANADA
DAY 4 — — — — —   GRANADA ~ MULHACÉN ~ GRANADA
DETOUR 4b —·—·—·—   MULHACÉN ~ *Lanjarón* ~ GRANADA

Granada

Arrive in Málaga.

I suggest you aim to arrive in Málaga the night before you begin to follow this tour.

Foreign visitors no longer flock to Málaga, preferring to view it as an easy gateway into other, more familiar names on the modern Costa del Sol. Yet a century ago the town was a fashionable resort for the monied middle classes of Europe, with a thriving expatriate English community. One relic of these days is instantly obvious: the horsedrawn carriages which continue to ply their trade around the gardens of the Paseo del Parque, now ringed with busy traffic. Málaga has no great attractions but, since it must be navigated on the way from the airport, it is worth taking a look at a city which has a roughshod charm for the regular visitor.

There are two ways of reaching Granada from Málaga, the fastest being the signposted route along the N321. This is a pleasant enough journey, and there is one spectacular view at Loja where the road runs above the interesting old 16th-century town. For those with time, however, there is a much more rewarding way, along the C335 by Vélez Málaga, to the east of Málaga itself. This diversion also offers a good chance to enjoy the sights of Málaga without the traffic problems which can beset a head-on approach to the city.

In Málaga, follow the signs for the main road to Almería, the N340, which leads past the port and then by the side of the lush tropical gardens of the Parque. At the end of the Parque, take the road signposted for the Parador and Gibralfaro. This takes us onto the hill which overlooks the city. The fine Parador, which has quiet rooms and a good restaurant, is situated on the top of the hill. Parking is easy – which is more than can be said for most places in Málaga. From the top, the views are very photogenic, with the city's bullring providing an unmistakably Spanish feel to the scene. Running down the hill stand the remains of the Arabic castle, the Gibralfaro, built on a site which has been used for fortifications since Phoenician times.

From here there is a pleasant stroll down the hill to the most interesting quarter of the city. Walking down the hill, one meets the Alcazaba, a heavily restored Moslem construction on Roman foundations and a small archeological museum.

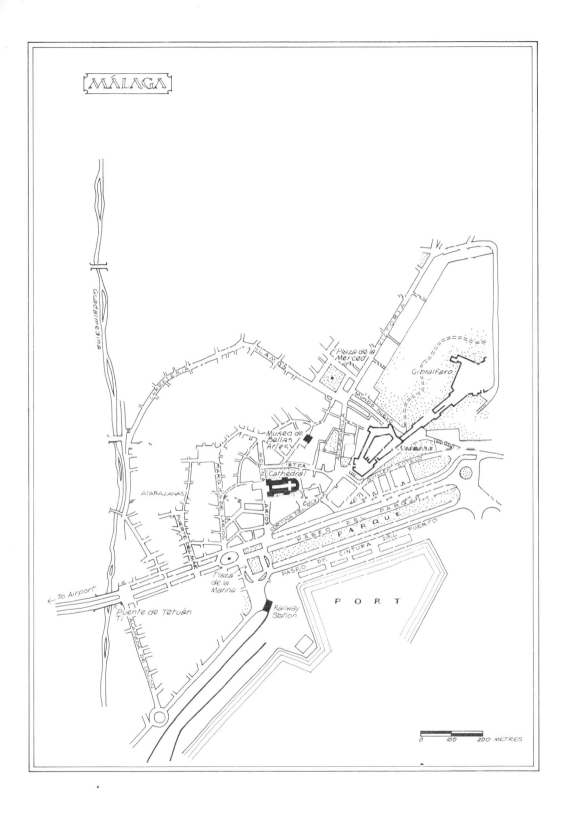

MÁLAGA

Guadalmedina

To Airport

Puente de Tetuán
Ti

ALAMEDA DE COLON

Plaza
de la
Marina

Railway
Station

PUENTE DEL MAR

ATARAZANAS

MARQUÉS DE LARIOS

MOLINA LARIO

CORTINA DEL MUELLE

Cathedral

BIBLIOTECA

Museo de
Bellas
Artes

ALAMOS

Plaza de la
Merced

MUNDO NUEVO

VICTORIA

Gibralfaro

GUILLEN DE CASTELO

PASEO DEL PARQUE

PARQUE

PASEO DE CINTURA DEL PUERTO

PORT

0   100   200 METRES

These are both rather insubstantial when compared against the sights ahead. It may be as well to take refreshment in the Parque before entering the cathedral.

A pause in these drowsy, tropical gardens, which lie between the foot of the hill and the sea, is always a pleasure, and there is not much cheer to be gained from the squat, unfinished hulk of the cathedral. It is the least interesting which we shall meet and I would recommend that it be avoided completely were it not for one wonderful asset: a 16th-century *coro* or carved wooden choir alive with scenes from the lives of the Catholic saints. The quality is not consistent, as one would expect in such a massive work which was handled by several artists. But it is a creation of great verve and beauty, and one for which this rather odd cathedral must be very grateful.

The diocesan museum is solely for those interested in church objects, but the Museo de Bellas Artes, which is indicated on leaving the cathedral, should not be missed. Málaga was Picasso's birthplace, as a plaque on the house in Plaza de la Merced testifies. For many the highlight of the museum is its collection of sketches, paintings and autographs of the artist stretching the distance of his long life.

The museum is housed in the Palacio de Buenavista, a substantial mansion with Arab antecedents, and the lover of old houses will gladly pay his entrance fee to step beyond its doors. In addition to the Picasso collection, there are works by Morales, Zurbarán, Murillo and Alonso Cano, and others of the great classical period of Spanish painting. The work of modern Andalucian painters, and those of local artists who influenced Picasso, complete the collection. It is the best gallery on this tour – Andalucia's two greatest being in the west at Cádiz and Seville – and a pleasant place to spend an hour or two.

Lunch may now be approaching – always a pleasant prospect in Málaga – but before retiring to the table there is one remaining curiosity which the city has to offer. There is a street called Atarazanas which leads off the busy road of Puerte del Mar – asking directions for the *mercado* or market will take you there quickly. Here we will find a square-fronted building with an attractive horseshoe arch door as its main entrance. This curiosity is the original entrance to the Arabic dockyards of the city, an indication of how far the sea has receded over the centuries. It is now part of the main market which is as fascinating as any on offer in a large Spanish city, with a particularly mouth-watering display of fish and crustacea – favourite foods in this maritime place.

Lunch in Málaga.

From Málaga, I prefer to follow the Almería highway east, through the Spanish seaside resort of Rincon de la Victoria to Torre del Mar where the road inland is marked for Vélez Málaga. The town appears on our right after a few miles. There are good views from the rebuilt castle which sits above the town but the traveller in a hurry to reach Granada will miss little by pressing on, into the hills of the Sierra de Tejeda which rise behind the coast. You will be passing tiny hill hamlets whose livelihoods are based upon the land, not the tourist industry.

Alhama de Granada

The setting of Alhama de Granada is often compared with that of the better known Ronda. Both communities are set on wild gorges, or *tajos*, and guide the visitor to the edge of the ravine. Unlike Ronda, Alhama is unused to tourists and one finds instead a rather reserved, traditional Spanish country town where one may wander observed by the puzzled residents. Outside, on the road to Granada, a cul-de-sac signposted to the Balncario leads to the baths which have attracted visitors for centuries to this remote health spa. The original Arab baths have been incorporated into a modern hotel and are modest in the extreme, but the countryside is idyllic and the amateur bird spotter will find much to interest him in the woods and fields.

Santafé

Granada is now fast approaching and you may, understandably, be getting impatient for your first view of this famed city. The town of Santafé which you pass after joining the main road from Málaga is a historic one, since it is based on the site of the army camp established by Ferdinand and Isabel for their final assault on Granada in 1492, the victory which was to unite Spain under a Christian monarchy and end almost eight centuries of Moslem influence. The foursquare ground plan of the centre of the town is said to mirror that of the tent encampments of the Christian forces. It is not a place suited to the modern motor car – park on the outskirts and walk into the centre.

35

Granada

Granada

We are now on the vega of Granada, the flat, fertile plain which is the source of the region's agricultural wealth, as the presence of roadside hawkers of citrus fruit and tomatoes testifies. It leads us into the unassuming suburbs of modern Granada. If you have decided to stay on the Alhambra, and I recommend that you do, follow the frequent signs that dot the city. When you are on the hill itself, ignore all attempts by apparently friendly locals to help you find a parking space – this is simply a local trick to fleece the gullible. A good hotel will take care of parking and provide any of the other services which the freelance hawkers of the hill may offer you.

Overnight in Granada.

ACCOMMODATION

Parador del Gibralfaro
Málaga
Tel: 221902

Undoubtedly the best place to stay in Málaga. A modern parador set at the top of the Gibralfaro hill, with quiet, comfortable rooms and good views. Fine restaurant serving local dishes.

Open all year
Rooms: 12
Facilities: terrace with views of the city
Credit cards: American Express, Diner's Club, Eurocard, Visa
Rating ****

Tropicana
Trópico 6
Torremolinos (four miles west of Málaga, two miles from airport)
Tel: 386600

Quiet hotel on the beach and close to the airport, suitable for an inexpensive overnight stay for anyone arriving late in the afternoon. La Carihuela, the old fisherman's district nearby, has many good seafood restaurants

Open all year
Rooms: 86
Facilities: private garden and beach club with outdoor pool
Credit cards: American Express, Diner's Club, Eurocard, Visa
Rating **

Granada

It is wise to stay in one of the hotels or hostels on the Alhambra Hill, since parking in the city is extremely difficult. There are regular buses from the Alhambra to the Plaza Nueva. Booking is essential during the summer, although the Doña Lupe can usually find a room at most times of the year or suggest somewhere else. Alternatively, for a quieter environment, one could stay in the village of Huétor Vega, three miles from the city centre, to which it is linked by regular buses.

Parador de San Francisco
Alhambra
Granada
Tel: 221440

One of the most famous of paradors, this is situated in an old monastery above the Charles V palace within walking distance of the main Alhambra sights. The building has been heavily restored and the rooms, while comfortable, lack ambience considering the surroundings. Its fame and popularity with international tourists make booking essential.

Open all year
Rooms: 39
Credit cards: American Express, Diner's Club, Eurocard, Visa
Food: dependable international cuisine for the largely tourist clientele
Rating *****

Alhambra Palace
Peña Partida 1
Granada
Tel: 221466

Luxury hotel in an interesting building at the edge of the hill, with fine views over the vega to the Sierra Nevada.

Open all year
Rooms: 133
Credit cards: American Express, Diner's Club, Eurocard, Visa
Food: unexciting upmarket tourist fare
Rating ****

Doña Lupe
Alhambra
Granada
Tel: 221474/221473

Comfortable rooms at low prices on the road to the Generalife make the Doña Lupe the best bargain on the Alhambra. The English-speaking proprietor is a fund of help and there is a pool on the roof.

Doña Lupe contd
Open all year
Rooms: 58
Credit cards: American Express, Diner's Club, Eurocard, Visa
Rating **

Mundo Nuevo
Huétor Vega (three miles from centre)
Tel: 500611

Hilltop hotel in village full of small restaurants popular with Granadino families. Quiet, comfortable rooms, a swimming pool, and spectacular views from all rooms.

Open April to October
Rooms: 12
Facilities: outdoor pool
Credit cards: American Express, Diner's Club, Eurocard, Visa
Rating **

EATING OUT

The Málaga region has a great love for fish, and fried fish in particular. The classic, almost clichéd, dish consists of slices of the freshest local fish perfectly fried. There are several variations. *Pescadillas* are small fish eaten whole, like whitebait, *fritura mixta* a selection of different fish, and *en adobo* sliced fillets, normally of bream (*dorada*) in a delicious, light garlic batter. Other popular fish varieties in the area are monkfish (*rape*), anchovies (*boquerones*), sardines grilled on a spit (*sardinas*), sole (*lenguado*), swordfish (*pez espada*), and red mullet (*salmonetes*). Large clams (*concha fina*) are eaten raw like oysters and are delicious.

There is an enormous selection of different kinds of prawns, from small gambas to large carabineros. Shellfish, and sometimes fried fish, are often sold by weight – ascertain how much a dish will cost before committing yourself, since seafood can be expensive.

The cold tomato and cucumber soup gazpacho is a common starter, but there is a delicious local variation, *ajo blanco*, made from ground almonds, garlic and grapes. Paella will only be worthwhile if it is made to order and expensive – in cheap restaurants it is inevitably made with yellow colouring, not saffron.

Restaurants in Granada are listed on p. 51-3.

Málaga

The best restaurants can be found close to the Parque, in the area around the Paseo de la Farole where there is a small beach popular with lunchtime bathers. There is a wide selection of *marisquerías* specialising in shellfish and numerous international restaurants.

Marisquería Mediterráneo
Paseo Marítimo 25
Málaga
Tel: 218497

One of the very best fish and seafood bars in Málaga, which is to say one of the best in Spain. Both fish and seafood are sold by weight on scales on the counter, enabling the diners to make their own selection from a range of prawns and fresh fish. There is an open kitchen with a grill on which whole bream sizzle *a la plancha* and delicate slices of *dorada* are fried *en adobo*.

Open all year, seven days a week
Credit cards: Visa, Eurocard
Rating **

Antonio Martin
Paseo Marítimo 4 (opposite the Marisquería Mediterráneo)
Málaga
Tel: 222113

There has been a restaurant with this name in Málaga for more than a century. There are few surprises on the menu, but the standard is always very high and there are outdoor tables by the sea.

Closed Sunday evenings in winter
Credit cards: American Express, Diner's Club, Eurocard, Visa
Rating ***

Torremolinos

Casa Juan
Calle Mes 16 (behind La Carihuela seafront)
Torremolinos

Small fisherman's bar with dining room serving first class seafood. *Conchas finas* are excellent; behind the bar is a large photograph of Torremolinos in 1957 when it was a small fishing village. *Dorada en adobo* particularly recommended.

Closed Mondays
No credit cards
Rating **

Marrakech
Ctra Benalmádena 7
Torremolinos
Tel: 382169

Genuine Moroccan restaurant close to the centre of town, with authentic tiled interior, North African music and clientele. Chicken pie with spices and sprinkled with sugar, *pastilla*, and a range of *couscous* and *tajine* are superb.

Closed Sundays
Credit cards: American Express, Diner's Club, Eurocard, Visa
Rating ***

MALAGA: USEFUL INFORMATION

Tourist office:	Paseo del Parque
	Tel: 228600
Population:	503,251
Facilities:	airport, bullring, passenger ferries
	to North Africa, and the
	Canary Islands

The Wine Gate, the Alhambra, Granada

DAY 2

A full day's walk around the city of Granada.

There is much more to the city of Granada than the famous Alhambra.
The best way to appreciate both Granada and the Alhambra is to spend
today in the city, then devote tomorrow fully to the palaces and gardens of
the Alhambra Hill. The local area around the Plaza de Bibirrambla makes
an interesting introduction to the city. Nearby street vendors sell herbs,
mountain delicacies and fresh fruit, then the walk continues into the old
Arabic hill community of the Albaicín, which stands opposite the
Alhambra Hill. In the afternoon, the Capilla Real, the Royal Chapel where
the coffins of Ferdinand and Isabel are on view, the Cathedral, the restored
silk market of the Alcaicería, and the original Arabic storehouse, the
Corral del Carbón, provide the opportunity to see many different facets of
Granadino culture within one small corner of the city.

Overnight in Granada.

Map reference
Granada   37° 10′N 3° 35′W

Breakfast in Granada.

Waking up on the Alhambra Hill, with the raggle-taggle golden complex of palaces beckoning through the woodland, the natural instinct is to race for the ticket booth and plunge into things immediately. After much thought, I have decided that the classical tour of the Alhambra is not the best way to start a visit to Granada. It can lead the newcomer to believe that there is no more to this gorgeous city than the palaces of long-dead Moslem rulers, now crowded with modern tourists. Once followed, one's instincts demand newer, even more impressive sights, and a whistlestop tour of Córdoba and Seville begins which leaves the mind a blur of Moslem architecture and Reconquest grandeur.

Granada deserves a gentler introduction, for much of its beauty stems from its happy ability to absorb its fascinating past while incorporating it into an equally stimulating present. It is a living city, not the well-preserved museum community which it might appear from certain angles. So let us begin our explorations by throwing history books to the wind.

Walk down from the Alhambra to the Plaza Nueva, the square where the road to the hill begins. Turning left you soon meet a broad thoroughfare running to the right – the Gran Via de Colón, one of the city's main arteries. Cross it at the pedestrian zone and then turn right until meeting the bluff walls of the cathedral. Iron gates on the left lead past ancient buildings which we shall investigate later – the most important being the Capilla Real, the Royal Chapel where Ferdinand and Isabel, the rather unlikely couple of joint monarchs who reconquered Spain for the Christian cause, are buried. Press on, past the Alcaicería, an interesting looking collection of small shops modelled on an Arabic bazaar, pausing only briefly at the local tourist office which appears on the left to collect a free map of the city and any topical publicity material on offer. Then a few steps more and we are in the Plaza de Bibirrambla, scene of bullfights, executions and festivals, and now the central square around which much of Granadino life is based.

If you have timed matters well it is around 9.30 in the morning and the city workers are making their final prevarications before facing up to the inevitability of working for the day. Early flower stallholders are surreptitiously sweeping rubbish onto their absent neighbour's patch, hopeful beg-

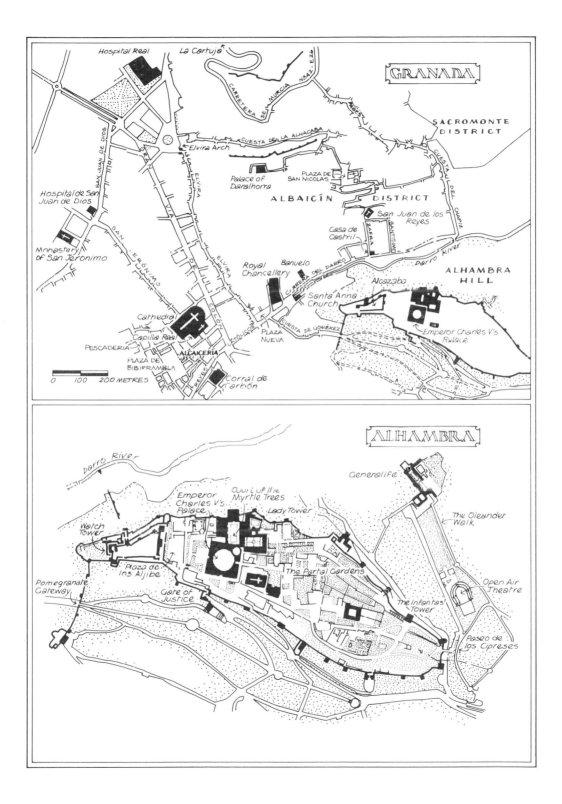

GRANADA

Hospital Real   La Cartuja

CARRETERA DE MURCIA N342-E24

SACROMONTE DISTRICT

CUESTA DE LA ALHACABA

Elvira Arch

SAN JUAN DE DIOS

Palace of Daralhorra   PLAZA DE SAN NICOLAS

ALBAICÍN   DISTRICT

CUESTA DEL CHAPIZ

Hospital de San Juan de Dios

SAN JERÓNIMO

San Juan de los Reyes

SANTISIMO

ZAFRA

Casa de Castril

Monastery of San Jerónimo

Darro River

ALHAMBRA HILL

Banuelo

Royal Chancellery

CARRERA DEL DARRO

Alcazaba

DE LA ELVIRA

COLÓN

Santa Anna Church

Cathedral

CUESTA DE GOMÉREZ

Capilla Real

Plaza Nueva

Emperor Charles V's Palace

PESCADERIA

PLAZA DEL BIBIRRAMBLA   ALCAICERÍA

REYES

CATÓLICOS

0   100   200 METRES

Corral de Carbón

ALHAMBRA

Darro River

Generalife

Emperor Charles V's Palace

Court of the Myrtle Trees

Lady Tower

The Oleander Walk

Watch Tower

Plaza de los Aljibe

The Partal Gardens

Pomegranate Gateway

Gate of Justice

Open Air Theatre

The Infantas' Tower

Paseo de los Cipreses

gars are trying to string together a convincing song for a few pesetas, and cafés everywhere are brimming with customers picking at churros, fresh doughnuts deep fried on the spot and dipped into glasses of strong black coffee, *café solo.*

Leave the square by the street of Pescadería, at the far right hand corner as you enter, and the first of a series of market stalls appears, selling everything from fresh fruit and vegetables to knives ground on the spot. At the end of Pescadería, on the left, is a small herb and spice shop which sells fresh saffron in sealed containers, an ideal and light purchase for anyone interested in regional cooking.

Cross the square which we now reach, following the avenue of palm trees into a busy narrow alley. Soon one is in the modern equivalent of an Arabic bazaar. City stallholders vie with peasants from the hills to sell everything from transistor radios to buckets of live snails raised in the mountains. Bunches of fresh herbs and wild asparagus are waved in the faces of hard-bargaining Granadino housewives. On the left a market building appears. Inside, on the ground floor, an enormous array of Mediterranean fish and shellfish glisten for the throngs of customers. Curiosity sated, return to the alley outside and continue until we are once more back at the Gran Via de Colón, where buses deposit commuters for their day's work and banks are opening their doors.

This small diversion taken by few visitors offers us an insight into the oriental heart beating beneath the modern face of Granada. Now let us head back to the Plaza Nueva and start our tour of the hillside district of Albaicín which stands opposite the Alhambra.

Begin at the Royal Chancellery, the elegant building we first saw when entering the Plaza from the Alhambra Hill and which, at the time of writing, is undergoing a substantial renovation. Continue past the chancellery and head for the narrow road, the Carrera del Darro, on the left. This picturesque street runs alongside the Darro river which goes underground at the Plaza Nueva. The church on the right, Santa Aña, is an interesting mixture of Moslem and Christian influences. The ornate front is in a Renaissance style known as Plateresque while the belltower is reminiscent of a minaret. Note the coloured tiles known as *azulejos* which lend the building an exotic air. All of these architectural features, Plateresque and

46

Moslem, are stylistic elements with which we will become familiar during our journey.

Passing the fashionable restaurant of Primer Puente, so named because it is close to the first bridge over the Darro, we come to a private house marked Banuelo, opposite the remains of an old Moslem gate into the city. The proud owner of the house will tell you that inside lie the best pre-served Arabic baths in Spain; many experts agree with her. The ceilings contain geometrically shaped vents and the columns show Roman and Byzantine origins. The heating arrangements and disrobing area are still obvious in what was probably a public bath for the Albaicín population, and consequently less ornate than those of the Alhambra Palace. There is no fixed entrance charge for your brief guided tour, but 100 pesetas per person would be appropriate.

Further along the street is the Casa de Castril, a Christian mansion with an elaborate Plateresque front which now houses the rich archeological museum. A brief excursion may be made here up the sidestreet of Zafra to the church of San Juan de los Reyes. This was the first church to be dedi-cated in Granada by the conquering Ferdinand and Isabel, so naturally it is a converted mosque, as is apparent from the minaret which now serves as a belltower. From the hill we have our first view of the Alhambra from the Albaicin. Return to the Darro by the path called Santisimo. On the right, after a small park, there is a diversion which leads to a muletrack rising into the Alhambra (this provides an alternative route to the Albaicín for those staying on the hill).

Follow the road called Cuesta del Chapiz which turns up the hill. On the right is the Historical Archive housed in a restored ducal palace surround-ed by well-tended gardens. Further up the hill there is a sign marking the Casas del Chapiz, two mansions which now house the school of Arabic studies. A polite chat with the doorkeeper will usually result in an invita-tion to walk round the lovely gardens which afford the best aspect of the Alhambra and the Generalife we have encountered so far.

There is a sign here to the district of Sacromonte, where gypsies live in caves and perform nightly dancing displays for gullible tourists. The quality of the dance is rarely more than mediocre and wallets are likely to be light-ened considerably in the exercise. Only the incorrigibly curious should venture further in this direction in the evening. The area is not dangerous, though there are the occasional bag snatchings one must expect in any big city, but the price of bad dancing can be surprisingly high.

Our next destination is the summit of the Albaicín itself. Cross the road from the Casas del Chapiz and take any of the paths leading uphill past pretty houses with abundant, sweet-smelling gardens.

Our destination, should you need to ask it of a passer-by, is the Plaza de San Nicolas. This open space in front of a plain, whitewashed church has, incontestably, the finest view of the Alhambra to be found anywhere in the city. The mass of the different palaces stands out in front of the snowy peaks of the Sierra Nevada, paler always in the morning than in the golden glow of the setting sun. The plaza draws locals and ambitious visitors alike throughout the day, many of whom sit for hours at a time enjoying this most memorable scene. It is also one more reason for placing one's visit to the Alhambra after that of the city. For the panorama from San Nicolas makes plain one of the Alhambra's remarkable truths: that this is a collection of palaces designed more for the delight of their occupants than the furtherance of military or political ambition. The Alhambra, seen from here, is not a grand exercise in state architecture, designed to impress – and intimidate – those who beheld it. Its purpose was more to delight the senses of its owner, as it delights ours today.

Leave the plaza by the unmarked road after the public library and the phone box and turn right at the end, through the old Arabic gate of the Puerta Nueva, into the Plaza Larga. We are now in the heart of the Albaicín's local quarter, where small street stalls can be found, the occasional horse will be exercised, and there are a couple of local cafés.

Return through the Puerta Nueva and bear right immediately after the gate, following the line of the old city walls. At a small park, keep to the right and soon the Palace of Daralhorra appears. A knock on the door and a 100 peseta tip gains entrance to the palace which was once the home of the mother of Boabdil, Granada's last Moorish king, By all accounts she was a formidable woman – when her son wept at abandoning the city she supposedly rebuked him with a cutting line which said, effectively, that he might as well cry like a woman since he never fought like a man.

The palace has a wealth of Moslem decoration which the caretaker insists, rather unconvincingly, has never been restored. Follow the Callejon del Gallo past rambling gardens and orchards little changed over the centuries. The Plazeta del San Miguel is a pleasant square; there are a handful of bars popular with Granadinos who want to escape the lunchtime rush and, in the evening, lamps light a crucifix at the centre. To the left is the Convent of Santa Isabel la Real now being restored.

Lunch in Granada.

Any of the narrow paths may be followed downhill. Eventually they will lead to the Plaza Nueva or the Gran Via de Colón, where we return in the afternoon to the Capilla Real and the cathedral. Of the two, the royal chapel is by far the most interesting. This was built as a mausoleum for the victorious monarchs Ferdinand and Isabel. Their small coffins can now be seen in a crypt underneath their marble effigies. The smaller figures by their side are those of their successor Juana, Isabel's unstable daughter who is still known as 'Joan the Mad', and her husband Philip of Burgundy.

The chapel has an intimacy rare in Spanish religious buildings and may be more to northern tastes than the baroque excesses seen in the neighbouring cathedral. Before rushing to examine the tombs, it is worth spending a few minutes at the back of the chapel admiring the enormous iron screen or *reja* which divides the building. This is considered to be one of the finest examples of reja work in the world, depicting heraldic emblems, biblical scenes and, finally, at its highest point, the Crucifixion.

Behind the tombs is a retablo in which Ferdinand and Isabel are depicted, on either side of the altar, preaching from lecterns, a practice which was unlikely to appeal to the wayward Ferdinand in life. A notorious womaniser and conspirator, Ferdinand's amoral attitude towards life and statesmanship stood in stark contrast to Isabel's relentless piety. Theirs was a remarkable political marriage of opposites. The king appears here by a panel depicting the fall of Granada in which the Alhambra is clearly recognisable, while Isabel is associated with the forcible conversion of Moslems. An ornate doorway leads into the treasury where Ferdinand's sword, Isabel's crown and jewel casket and the ceremonial robes of the couple may be seen. Many of the paintings are from the Flemish school which Isabel greatly favoured; these cool, almost dull, canvases reflect the pious, some-what tedious, character of this momentous queen.

Having ventured this far, it would be a mistake not to visit the cathedral itself, though the building is not among the city's abiding memories. The entrance is back in the Gran Via. After a small diocesan museum, one enters the vast and gloomy interior. Those with an interest in art will find works by the acclaimed Granadino painter and sculptor Alonso Cano, and others by Ribera and Montanes. It may be worthwhile to bring a small torch to illuminate detail in the poor light.

Leaving the cathedral, we have two final items on our itinerary – both of more cheer. The first is found on the left after the entrance to the Royal Chapel – the Alcaicería, or silk market, which we noticed on our morning walk. This is a small huddle of shops housed in what appears to be an Arabic market. Appearances are deceptive – the area was built in the last century when the cult of Arabic art was being revived in the city. They make a novel sight, however, though the assortment of tourist gewgaws and 'handicrafts' which they sell do little to whet the appetite.

Cross the main road from the Plaza Nueva and walk to the right to find a sign pointing to the Corral del Carbón which leads to a more genuine Arabic market. This is a 14th-century storehouse found at the top of a narrow alley. There is a wealth of ornamental work, most notably in the entrance arch and an attractive courtyard. After many different uses, the Corral is now the home of a handicraft organisation which specialises in the kind of furnishings and other craftwork which will appeal to wealthy, well-travelled collectors, a far cry from the Alcaicería indeed.

Dinner and overnight in Granada.

ACCOMMODATION, see p. 37-9.

EATING OUT

Granada looks to the mountains for its culinary influences, not the coast. While fresh fish is available in many restaurants, the true Granadino dish is marked by mountain ham and beans from the vega. A traditional *plato granadino* will normally be a hearty plate of fried eggs and beans with ham and sausage. A speciality of the city is the *tortilla Sacromonte*, an omelette made with lamb, potatoes, brains, red pepper and peas which appears on menus everywhere but is rarely of much interest. Granada likes to feel it is a fashionable city and has lately developed a taste for modern restaurants serving dishes based on nouvelle cuisine. Such establishments appear and disappear so quickly that it is impossible to record them on paper. But be prepared to follow if you see the equivalent of a Granadino yuppie entering what appears to be his favourite eating house.

Sevilla
Oficios 12
Granada
Tel: 221223

This is a Granadino institution close to the entrance of the Capilla Real, serving local dishes such as *tortilla Sacromonte* and good fish and ham. Tapas may be taken in the bar while the restaurant has a dining room and, in summer, tables on the pavement. Deservedly popular with the locals, with friendly, helpful staff.

Closed Sunday night
Credit cards: American Express, Diner's Club, Eurocard, Visa
Rating ***

Cunini
Pescadería 9
Granada
Tel: 263701

Traditional restaurant specialising in fish with a busy *marisquería* attached.

Cunini contd
The cooking is reliable, service somewhat dour. The trout à la Navarre (*trucha Navarra*) is interesting: the fish is stuffed with mountain ham.

Open every day
Credit cards: American Express, Diner's Club, Eurocard, Visa
Rating ***

Alberto
Alhambra
Granada
Tel: 224818

Terrace restaurant near the road to the Generalife, serving grill dishes with summer tables in the garden. Probably the best bet on the Alhambra.

Closed Thursdays
Credit cards: American Express, Diner's Club, Eurocard, Visa
Rating ****

Cafétin La Porrona
Plaza Larga 4
Granada

Friendly local bar/restaurant in the centre of the Albaicín serving whatever the chef has bought for the day. No menu, no phone, lots of atmosphere.

Open every day
No credit cards
Rating **

Alacena de Las Monjas
Plaza del Padre Suárez 5
Granada
Tel: 224028

Elegant and arty modern cuisine with tables in old cellars, populated by fashionable Granadinos. Highly imaginative and largely successful food:

Alacena de Las Monjas contd
leeks with almonds and cheese, pastel of aubergine and salmon, red peppers stuffed with salt cod in a saffron sauce.

Closed Sundays and Mondays
Credit cards: American Express, Diner's Club, Eurocard, Visa
Rating ***

For local tapas try El Fogon, in Calle Angel Ganivet, near the Puerta Real. This bullfighting tavern serves an excellent range of local dishes and hams. Bodegas La Mancha, in Calle Joaquin Costa, off Calle Reyes Catolicos, is a working class tapas bar with a busy food counter: try the *lomo*, pork fillet slices grilled to order.

GRANADA: USEFUL INFORMATION	
Tourist office:	Libreros, 2
	Tel: 225990
Population:	262,182
Facilities:	domestic airport

The Lion Court, the Alhambra, Granada

DAY 3

A walking tour of the Alhambra.

The palaces and gardens of the Alhambra Hill are explored on a full day's walk. The chapter covers the whole of the Alhambra, beginning at the Puerta de las Granadas, then moving through the Puerta de la Justicia to the old fortress of the Alcazaba, the Renaissance palace of Charles V, the sumptuous Moslem royal quarters of the Palacios Nazaries, the living area of the court families, and finally the famous Generalife gardens.

Overnight in Granada.

Map reference
Granada   37° 10´N 3° 35´W

Breakfast in Granada.

'Alhambra, Alhambra!' shout the gypsies looking for business in Granada's most famous attraction. The magic words are designed to stop the passing traveller – and his wallet – in his tracks just by their very sound. Yet there is no single entity we can call 'the Alhambra', but a multitude of buildings and gardens from different centuries which today exist under the collective name of the hill on which they stand.

Before exploring these separate yet connected parts, it is worth setting out their identities so that we can recognise them as they appear. The traditional entrance to the Alhambra is via the Cuesta de Gomeres in the Plaza Nueva. At the time of writing, this represents the only route onto the hill by car; to leave you must take an exit road through the Antequeruela, the hillside district which lies beneath the Alhambra Palace Hotel and is, in its own way, as fascinating as the Albaicín explored yesterday.

There are many development plans in hand for the Alhambra which, before the turn of the century, seem certain to ban cars and coaches from some of the parts which they now choke, and to build a new entrance and exit route into the hill from the east. When this happens, the Cuesta de Gomeres will remain the principal entrance – through the happy medium of an electric tram – and one will continue to arrive through the Renaissance gateway of the Puerta de las Granadas which sits a few hundred yards up the hill. It is not, it must be said, the most propitious of first sights, since the gate reflects nothing whatsoever of the buildings which you are about to see. The most interesting aspect of the construction is its depiction of the fruit associated with the city for centuries – the pomegranate or *granadino*. Nor is the association limited to Spanish – as the French *grenadine* or pomegranate syrup indicates.

From the Puerta de las Granadas, a public road winds to the head of the hill where the little-visited fort of the Sillo del Moro stands, reputedly the place to which the unfortunate Boabdil retired when the fall of the city to the Christians became inevitable. To the right there are ruins of the city walls, known as the Torres Bermejas, and to the left the complex of palaces which make up what we generally know as the Alhambra. Above these stands the Generalife, the Moslem ruler's private pleasure ground which has now been converted into extensive and beautiful gardens best known for the music festival which they host each June.

The Alhambra is a unique experience which deserves to be approached with forethought and patience. You will find it's like nowhere else in the world. No North African city possesses such finery of decoration, no European city such a wealth of Moslem architecture.

A few practical matters require attention before tackling the substantial task before us, however, since, without care, all of these wonderful sights may flash past in a disorganised blur. The seasoned Alhambra visitor – and there are many who return again and again – may be recognised by four characteristics: a sound pair of well-soled canvas shoes, an expression of worldweariness, a large shoulder bag, and a trained weather eye forever watching the movements of large parties of package tourists negotiating the hill en masse. The first two are local considerations; canvas shoes with good soles serve the dual purpose of being both light and comfortable during the heavy walking ahead and discouraging the roving armies of bootblacks who will pounce on a pristine leather upper the moment its owner slows below three miles per hour.

A languid expression, preferably matched by a reasonable suntan, may feign Spanish nationality sufficiently to deter a few of the wandering gypsies trying to thrust a single carnation into the hands of the unwary with professions of undying love and a promise that the bloom is for free (testaments both of which are rarely, if ever, borne out in reality). A capacious shoulder bag should provide space for a day's books, camera, film and, if you are feeling adventurous, a few morsels for a makeshift picnic in any of the splendid terraces which we shall meet along the way. And our last attribute may be the most important of all – for, as we have discussed, the Alhambra remains a Mecca for the modern tourist. Step into the wrong doorway at the wrong time and you may find yourself swept along by a tide of giggling pensioners from Perpignan from the Mexuar audience hall clean into the gardens of the Partal on the other side of the royal palaces. The Alhambra knows no off-season – though it is certainly at its busiest in the middle of the summer. With a little cunning, however, it is perfectly easy to negotiate the whole of the hill at your own pace, and in relative peace, at any time of the year.

Let us begin at a slightly awkward point for those who have taken my advice and decided to stay on the Alhambra Hill itself. The road from the Plaza Nueva leads directly into the heart of the Alhambra and, as we arrive from most of the popular hotels, the obvious route would seem to be to follow the cars. Resist, and head further downhill to the large gate, the Puerta de la Justicia, where coaches disgorge their customers. This provides us with a view of the genuine entry route into the Alhambra – a little further down the hill you can still see the ruins of another gate, the Bibirrambla, and if you wait for the crowds to clear you will understand why this makes a sensible entry point. The imposing gate, with the enormous horseshoe arch at its centre, was the place where the ordinary visitor to Moslem Granada would have discovered whether he was fit to enter the palace or not. Here high officials vetted arriving merchants and supervised the execution of criminals.

To the right, as you approach, there is a small fountain dedicated to the memory of the American author Washington Irving whose writing, in the first half of the last century, helped drag the Alhambra out of the ruinous state into which it had fallen. Irving stayed in the Alhambra, then largely a tenement complex, and turned its many myths into a bestseller of the day, *Tales of the Alhambra*. The interest which this stimulated raised funds for the renovation which we can enjoy today.

Above the gateway is a statue of the Virgin and Child which the visitor may find curious in a gate which is composed of largely Moslem decorations. This combination of Christian and Islamic art is one to which we will grow accustomed, however. After the Reconquest, it was impossible for the Christians to destroy nearly five centuries of Moslem influence, though there were those who tried. Moslem craftsmen were frequently employed to create Islamic masterpieces by their Christian overlords, sometimes slipping Arabic texts into the complex patterns which typify their work. This style of Moslem art created under Christian rule is so common that it has earned a name of its own – *mudéjar* – and we shall meet it many times on this journey.

Walk through the gate, noting the interior turns designed to aid its defence in hand-to-hand fighting, and follow the signs for the sale of tickets. At the top of the path, we turn through the Puerta del Vina to see a large and unexpected Renaissance building ahead of us and, to our right, the busy ticket office which can also supply maps and detailed guidebooks. A word of warning about the Alhambra ticket – it works on a one-way basis. Once you have used your portion for a part of the hill, there is no re-entry. Often populated by noisy and energetic swifts, the 12th-century Puerta del Vina is one of the oldest structures in the Alhambra. Through it we reach the first part of our tour and a small café with views over the town. It is worth considering, at this stage, the different elements into which the Alhambra may be divided.

The first and oldest part stands to our left as we face the Albaicín. This is the Alcazaba, a fortress which resembles many still found in southern Spain. To our right, as we look at the Albaicín, the royal palaces – where the most gorgeous halls and patios are to be found – lie closest to the outer wall. Behind it stand the buildings of the Christian rulers, the Palace of Charles V, the large Renaissance building we saw when entering, the church of Santa Maria la Real, which is of no interest to the casual visitor, and a conglomeration of shops which lead to the parador of San Francisco. Behind the church lies the quarter where the senior officials of the ruler's household lived – the Población – now a handsome garden complex revealing the foundations of old houses and known as the gardens of the Partal. Above us, hidden from view, is the Generalife. Our ticket includes entrance to each of these elements of the Alhambra.

One insight which no ticket can provide is a clue to what everyday life was like in the Alhambra from the 12th to the 15th century when it was a true Moslem palace. The general functions of the sections of the palace can be seen from the layout of the complex today – the fortifications, the quarters for the civil servants, and the ruler's private palace. The love of ornament, gardens and water indicate the state of mind of the Moslems who created these palaces. They were not severe, authoritarian people, but pleasure-lovers, fond of the proverbial wine, women and song. Poets and artists were court favourites, and beneath the main palace was a substantial harem from which the ruler would choose his companion for the night. The Alhambra was rarely without its intrigues, and these occasionally spilled over into bloodshed. But in essence, the hill was a pleasure garden for a hedonistic court fond of temporal delights. To the more devout and puri-tanical Moslems of North Africa, particularly the Almohads who overran Seville in the 12th century, court life of Moslem kingdoms like Granada was nothing short of a public scandal.

We begin at the Alcazaba. Charting a reliable way around the monument is difficult; constant renovation – something we shall always meet in the Alhambra – and excavations dictate that different paths are followed on different years. The key elements remain the same, however. A climb to the top of the tallest tower, the Torre de la Vela, is essential for the lovely views of the city. You can retrace your steps of yesterday through the Albaicín and cast a disapproving look at the squat mass of the cathedral down below.

In the distance we can see the snow on the Sierra Nevada and, stretching from the city, the vega, the rich, fertile plain which supports the prosperous agricultural industry. On close examination, you will also be able to see fellow sightseers on the Plaza de San Nicolas, which we visited yesterday, staring back across the valley of the Darro.

The central part of the Alcazaba, the Barrio Castrense, reveals much foundation work and the dank, subterranean cells of slaves, presumably Christian in the main, who provided the labour for the palace complex. Walk through into the Adarve garden, at the back of the Alcazaba, from where one may see the Torres Bermejas from a delightful patio of flowers and trees. The poem inscribed as we enter is one of the most famous about the city; it translates – *give him alms, woman, for there is nothing in life to match the grief of being blind in Granada.*

After the Alcazaba one should examine the Palace of Charles V. From the outside we see an imposing stone mass of perfect geometric proportions. Elsewhere, it would be more admired as a great Renaissance building; here it can only stand, metaphorically, in the shadow of the earlier Moslem palaces. Enter the door and one is immediately taken aback, for the interior is not the network of large halls expected but a circular space open to the sky, similar to a bullring, a purpose to which it has been put. The proportions seem even more exact than the exterior, and the curve of the handsome stone resembles the precise shaping of some natural organism more than the work of a human architect. The precise purpose of the building remains a matter of debate. It was originally intended as a royal palace, to replace the draughty corridors of the Alhambra during winter (which visitors in January will appreciate).

Upstairs is the Museo de Bellas Artes which demands a small extra fee. The

gallery is of principally parochial interest and prone to a process of perpet-
ual *reformación* and *restauración* which means that it is extremely difficult to
predict with any accuracy what you will be able to see. This is no uncom-
mon occurrence in Spain, as you may discover for yourself, but Granada
seems more adept at the practice than other areas.

The most interesting works are by two very different Granadinos, the monk
Sánchez Cotán and the rather less austere Alonso Cano, an artist whose life
was truly bohemian throughout. Cotán's best work is in his still life depictions of everyday food which are far more exciting than they sound. He is
well represented at La Cartuja, the 17th-century monastery which lies
behind the Albaicín, where he worked. Cano was of deeper stuff and, cru-
cially, trained in Seville when the city was producing its greatest artists. His
dark, emotional canvases may be compared with Cotán's brightly lit and
rather unsubstantial religious works here. You can see not just the difference in temperaments of two artists but that of two cities as well.

After this brief trip into the Renaissance, we must tackle the masterpiece of
the Alhambra, the royal palaces themselves. The entrance, marked by a
sign for the Palacios Nazaries, is back through the Puerta del Vina and
here, most of all, one must take care not to become sandwiched between
two coach groups moving at a snail's pace. We walk through a patio garden
into the original audience hall of the palace, the Mexuar, where there is
much stucco work and Arabic inscription, some of it restored and, in the
corner an oratory for Moslem prayer. Turning to the right, we enter the
Patio of the Mexuar with, to our left, a separate chamber, the Cuarto
Dorado with lovely views of the Albaicín hill. In the centre of the patio
stands a low fountain, the first of a series of water features which run
throughout the palaces.

The route now leads into a large, open hall with a fish pool along much of
its length, the Patio de los Arrayanes. This sunny patio offers a glimpse of
the beauty which the original Arab architects must have sought in their
work. There is a profusion of scripts and patterns around the walls, and an
atmosphere of calm and joy, even at the busiest of times. To our left,
through a small room known as the Sala de la Barca, we enter what is probably the single most lovely small chamber in the whole of the Alhambra,
the Sala de Embajadores. The chamber, set inside the palace's largest
tower, is open on three sides – though glass has now been added for the

comfort of visitors – and looks out upon much of the city. The fourth view, through the entrance, is almost as exquisite, marred only by the addition of an extra storey at the rear of the Patio de los Arrayanes during the construction of the Charles V palace. The combination of horseshoe arches of many different sizes and the continuous wall decoration are reflected in the still waters where black goldfish swim lazily.

A small door on the left, as we come from the Sala de Embajadores, leads into the Sala de los Mocarabes, with an out of place Renaissance ceiling, and then to the Patio de los Leones, which is perhaps the best known image of the Alhambra for those who so far have only read about the place. The name stems from the fountain at its centre, where 12 elegant lions support the central basin. A forest of 124 columns supports the hall, lending it a fairytale air which at first almost defies belief. Go round anticlockwise, reaching first the Sala de los Abencerrajes where you will normally find a coach party being enthralled by an enthusiastic guide. It was here, according to local tradition, that the leaders of the Abencerrajes were summoned individually by Boabdil's officials and beheaded one by one during the feuding which preceded the fall of the city.

Traces of red on the fountain are frequently cited as the victims' blood, though you will see them on other fountains in the palace and they look very much like rust to this observer. The room has much fascinating detail and a lovely ceiling. The arches of the patio reflect in the waters of the fountain at certain angles, and the most garrulous of visitors are silenced by the stillness.

At the rear of the patio is the Sala de los Reyes, the king's private quarters where, as one might expect, the stucco work is at its most sumptuous. A curiosity of this hall is the series of westernised paintings on leather which can be seen in alcoves at the rear. That in the centre depicts the Moslem kings of Granada, none of whom looks remotely Arabic. The last adjoining hall, the Sala de Dos Hermanas, lies opposite that of the Abencerrajes and is most noted for its intricate stalagmite ceiling and more lovely views of the Albaicín and the gypsy quarter of Sacromonte to the right.

The patio of the lions is the last section of this central part of the Alhambra and there is no turning back once you have left the exit in the Sala de los Reyes. The door connects with the Gardens of the Partal, part of the

Población or living area of the palace household. Foundations of houses arc still to be seen throughout the modern gardens, and one exquisite house, the Torre de las Damas, remains. It is found to our left as we enter the gardens, in front of it lies an enormous pool. Adjoining it are the few remaining workmen's houses from Moslem times.

An entrance underneath the palace we have just visited leads into the Daraxa Garden. Attached to this are parts of the Arab baths which were an integral part of the palace. The room closest to the central section of the palace was probably attached to the ruler's harem.

At this stage, the visitor is probably ready for lunch, or a drink and sandwich at the very least. There is a small snack bar at the top of the Partal gardens. If you would like to eat in one of the Alhambra's restaurants you must leave the palace complex. The short way is by the exit close to the Charles V palace; the long way involves following the walls of the Alhambra around the hill, passing several towers in the course of restoration, and leaving by the large Alhambra car park close to the old road to the cemetery. Alberto's, see p. 52, is a little way down the hill.

Either way your ticket to the Generalife will remain valid for the afternoon. The Generalife requires little by way of explanation. This was the palace pleasure garden and now, appropriately, it serves the same function in its restored form for the modern visitors who enjoy the Alhambra. Many of the buildings have been heavily restored and cannot hope to match the palace itself.

The gardens, tended by a permanent army of labourers, are memorable throughout the year for their profusion of colours and the fountains and channels of water which run throughout their length. Each June the Generalife is the scene of a popular classical music festival which attracts regular visitors from all over Europe for its combination of sound and surroundings.

No detailed guide is required for the Generalife – follow your instincts and explore.

Overnight in Granada.

Accommodation and restaurants, see pp. 37-9 and pp. 51-3.

Sierra Nevada

DAY 4

An excursion to the Sierra Nevada, of around 55 miles, followed by a visit to some of the remaining sights in Granada.

The mountains of the Sierra Nevada, permanently capped by snow, make a vivid background to the Alhambra. The highest road in Europe leads to the summit and, in the summer months for the adventurous driver, over into the Alpujarra. In the afternoon, several of the remaining sights in the city may be seen, including the house of the poet Federico Garcia Lorca and a museum dedicated to his memory. The Elvira Arch, one of the old Moslem gates to the city, the Hospital Real, the monasteries of Cartuja and San Jeronimo and the Hospital de San Juan de Dios are among the historic buildings which are often overlooked.

Overnight in Granada.

Route shown p. 30.

Map references

Granada	37° 10´N 3° 35´W
Veleta	37° 04´N 3° 22´W
Mulhacén	37° 03´N 3° 19´W
Huétor Vega	37° 33´N 3° 33´W
Pinos Genil	37° 10´N 3° 30´W
Prado Llano	37° 08´N 3° 25´W

Granada

Breakfast in Granada.

It feels distinctly odd to see, for the first time, a pair of skis bobbing through the rush hour traffic of Granada on a hot spring day when thoughts are turning to the coast and the sea. But, as you soon discover, this is a fashionable city, and the fashion for the last decade or so has been to ski, as visibly as possible, throughout each winter on the slopes of the Sierra Nevada.

A new ski resort, Prado Llano, reached by the highest road in Europe, has sprung up to cater for the demand, and ski lifts, a wide range of small restaurants of different nationalities, and several hotels with the curious modern architecture peculiar to the winter sports fraternity now operate from late autumn to early spring.

For the average visitor, with no desire to launch himself down the slopes, the journey to the Sierra Nevada remains worthwhile, for the countryside through which we will pass and the views from close to the summits of the two principal peaks, Veleta (3,800 feet) and Mulhacén (3,806 feet). The journey is relatively easy and will occupy a morning.

For the very adventurous there is the opportunity to cross the Sierra Nevada itself into the Alpujarra. The main mountain road turns into a stony track which leads over Mulhacén and descends into Bubión. From here, one may return by the pretty road to Granada through Lanjarón, or leave Granada altogether and pursue this itinerary in reverse, beginning at Day Eleven which covers the Alpujarra. A strong word of warning should be given about this road, however. It is only open during the height of the summer, and the track is narrow, circuitous and daunting. A four wheel drive car is advisable and it is best to seek the advice of your hotel before planning to take it.

One leaves the Alhambra by the Antequeruela, the district which runs from the height of the hill to the Genil river. Its most famous inhabitant was the composer Manuel de Falla whose house is preserved, with a con-cert auditorium. At the foot of the hill, follow the signs for the Sierra Nevada, doubling back on the Carrera del Genil in order to leave the city. In the centre of the dual carriageway you will see an old yellow tram pre-served from the days when they were the principal form of public transport. More modern means of traffic congestion have now been invented, as you will already have discovered. A minor road to the right to Huétor Vega makes an interesting detour for those with the time. This growing village of the vega is a popular destination for Granadinos at the weekends who flock to its fine local restaurants and take country walks.

A sign reminds us that we are heading for the highest road in Europe, the GR420, though to be honest it can scarcely be described as hard driving even into the very peaks of the sierra, and an electronic billboard gives an indication of the weather on the summit. The road follows the line of the Genil valley through orchards and past a series of popular roadside inns, then, at the picturesque village of Pinos Genil begins to make its serious ascent of the range.

Prado Llano

The white peaks become visible ahead of us and snow warning signs appear. There are several miradors marked here, official stopping points which afford good views of the surrounding landscape. Miradors have been created throughout Spain and are usually well signposted, with parking facilities and, on occasion, a small café. From these it is possible to see the route to Granada below and some of the aqueducts, dating from Moslem times, which were built to channel water from the peaks into the city. Prado Llano fits into its environment as well as most ski resorts, that is to say not at all. A haphazard array of odd shaped hotels cling together on the bare mountainside housing, during the winter, a cheery international community. When the snow disappears so do they, leaving the place a ghost town for much of the summer. Nor is the skiing much of a challenge for the serious winter sports enthusiast, though it has little competition in this part of the world.

There is a local boast that it is possible to ski at Prado Llano in the morning and then drive to the Mediterranean to swim in the afternoon. Quite why anyone should want to perform such an odd combination of activities is something which has never been explained to me, but doubtless it will appeal to some.There is a parador here, a low, wooden hotel above Prado Llano to which it is linked by a ski lift and the road which continues on towards the summit of Veleta. It is open throughout the year for coffee and food. During the summer a surprising number of walkers book into the hotel, and the surrounding, cheaper, albergues, to spend a few days of absolute solitude wandering across the bare peaks.

The weather will dictate how far you may progress from here. Even into June, snow drifts may block the road some way before the peak of Veleta, causing an odd little traffic jam of cars, motorbikes and campers trying to make U-turns on the narrow road. The fortunate will be able to press beyond the popular skiing zone, which ends at Veleta, towards Mulhacén. Footpaths lead to the peak, and that of neighbouring La Alcazaba.

There is an incomparable panorama of the whole region, from the coast and the Alpujarra to Granada and the vega. On the return it is best to avoid lunch in Prado Llano and try, instead, one of the tiny roadside inns, with rather unpredictable opening hours and a marked dislike for credit cards, which serve true sierra food. La Higuera, just before the turning to Purche, is typical, with home-raised chicken and the ever-popular *choto*, mountain kid, served at very low prices.

The people of the mountains are great, if small-scale, entrepreneurs, ever ready to offer jars of delicious honey and a range of lovely fruit from their gardens to the passer-by. Casual inquiries in Pinos Genil can also afford the opportunity for a spot of coarse fishing or even a little hunting.

The afternoon may be used to see a few more of Granada's lesser-known sights. It is impossible to visit everywhere of interest in a few days, since this is a large and complex city best explored over several visits. However, I shall list here some of the principal sights which we have not covered. It impossible to leave Granada without mentioning the poet Federico Garcia Lorca, the greatest Spanish writer of this century, who was murdered by the Nationalists in his home town during the Civil War.

Lorca was a true Granadino; the city and its spirit runs through virtually all of his work:

'In this town I had my first dream of remoteness. In this town I will be earth and flowers. Its streets, its people, its customs, its poetry and its wickedness will be as the scaffold where my childhood ideas will nest and melt in the fire of my puberty.'

A museum has been established in his memory in the house where he was born in Fuentevaqueros on the city outskirts, and it is also possible to visit the family mansion, La Huerta. Opening times and arrangements are fluid and it is best to book a visit in advance through the tourist office near the Plaza de Bibirrambla.

There is much of interest in the north of the city, at the end of the Gran Via. Here you will find the Elvira Arch, one of the original city gates, and the Hospital Real, a beautiful renaissance building which now houses the university. Close by is La Cartuja, the monastery which is, perhaps, best known for its collection of Cotán paintings, and more remains of early Moslem walls. To the west lie the Hospital de San Juan de Dios and the charming, if somewhat scruffy, Monastery of San Jeronimo.

In the latter lies the body of one of Spain's most famous warriors, Gonzalo Fernandez de Córdoba, known always as el Gran Capitan. There is a statue of him in the oddly garish church and decorations which link him with every other hero in history which the commissioned artists could think of. In another world, where Granada possessed no Alhambra, the patio of this monastery would be restored to pristine condition and prove one of the city's great attractions. It is a measure of how much there is to distract the eye in Granada that this lovely courtyard is largely neglected, and visited, in the main, only by parties of Spanish schoolchildren on history lessons.

Overnight in Granada.

Accommodation and restaurants, see pp. 37-9 and pp. 51-3.

Alcalá la Real

DAY 5

From Granada to Córdoba, around 120 miles.

The route follows the main road until Alcalá la Real, with its imposing hill-side fort, then branches through pretty countryside to Priego de Córdoba. There is a stop at Montilla, famous in Spain for its local wines, before arriving in Córdoba.

Overnight at Córdoba.

Route shown p. 90.

Map references

Granada	37° 10´N 3° 35´W
Pinos Puente	37° 15´N 3° 48´W
Alcalá la Real	37° 30´N 3° 58´W
Almedinilla	37° 28´N 4° 05´W
Priego de Córdoba	37° 28´N 4° 15´W
Córdoba	37° 52´N 4° 45´W

Granada

Breakfast in Granada.

There is a good, fast road from Granada to Córdoba and, like most of its
kind, it tends to skirt the towns it meets, often leading the visitor away from
places which would otherwise provoke some interest.

We leave Granada by the Gran Via de Colón, following the signs for Málaga
and the N323. Just outside the city there is a branch to the right, signposted for Córdoba on the N432. Heavy traffic is common on the exit route
from the city, so an early start is advisable. Some five miles from the
Hospital Real we arrive at the small town of Pinos Puente which has nothing to indicate that it provides a worthwhile stop for the passing visitor.

Pinos Puente

As you enter the town there is a sharp bend to the left. Take the junction to
the right here and then park after a few hundred yards near the bus stop.
At the end of the street on the left we find a most curious bridge, with a
white chapel straddling it, several plaques and a bust of an unrecognisable
figure. The fruit and flower sellers seem largely oblivious to any sense of
history in the spot, yet this is a place which merits a mention in most
Spanish school textbooks.

The bridge itself is unusual, predating the Arabic invasion. Its creators
were probably the Visigoths, those argumentative Christians whose feuding
did much to make the task of the eighth-century Arab invaders so easy.
Beneath the bridge a small stream meanders stocked, in summer, with
vociferous frogs; the main waters have been diverted to a higher level.

It was here, or so the history books have it, that Christopher Columbus
decided to return to Granada to make one more attempt to plead with
Ferdinand and Isabel to support the expedition to the New World. Had he
not, then the historic expedition might have been made under the banner
of England or France, which may explain the weight the Spanish history
books place upon this place. A plaque commemorates the event and the
bust is of Columbus, known in Spain as Cristóbal Colón. Spain abounds in
apocryphal tales such as these, of course, and it is worth bearing in mind
that several places, Granada and Santafé among them, claim the honour of
being the spot where Columbus and Isabel actually signed the agreement
to launch the expedition.

One must remember that the Catholic monarchs had rather larger matters in hand than the financing of outlandish expeditions. For them, 1492 was the year which marked the Reconquest of the whole of Spain with the fall of Granada, and it is only history which has shifted the significance of the year to mark it as the one in which Columbus 'sailed the ocean blue'.

From Pinos Puente we follow the road north, rising into the mountains of Jaen province which at times may appear to be one vast olive plantation. Nowhere else in Spain is the humble olive so widely grown or admired, and the Jaen farmer will happily chatter for hours on the health-giving properties of its products.

Alcalá la Real

On the horizon appears the vast fortress of the Fortaleza de la Mota which stands over the town of Alcalá la Real. This is a handsome castle, though it is hard to point to any items inside which will remain in the memory, much as the local handbooks try. You will find it signposted to the left as you drive through the town. From the walls one can appreciate how important the olive is to the local economy. The lines of trees march out in every direction, sending the mind reeling to calculate how any nation could consume so many millions of olives. They stretch north in this fashion for a good 60 miles to Andújar and beyond and, as farmers happily admit, are uncountable.

At the end of Alcalá, bear left to follow the sign for Priego de Córdoba, thus leaving the main route to Córdoba and joining a pleasant and excellent country road, the C336, which crosses into Córdoba province, eventually linking with the main road from Málaga to Córdoba, the N331, at Monturque.

Almedinilla

In the hills we come across the small village of Almedinilla, the white rooftops visible from a distance. Moved some sixty miles to the south, this would inevitably earn the dread description 'typical' and attract hundreds of Costa del Sol tourists daily, all looking for Andalucian rural life at its most authentic. Fortunately, Almedinilla has been spared this fate by geography and is simply a charming hillside village with many picturesque aspects and a couple of cafés which are welcome breaks from the wheel.

Priego de Córdoba

The larger town of Priego de Córdoba now appears on the horizon, peering from behind a white battlement. Priego is as ignorant of the tourist as its larger namesake is knowing, and there is little in the way of conventional facilities, though a couple of cafés will make fine jamón serrano sandwiches for a filling lunch. From the ramparts which we saw from a distance, there is a fine view of the route we have followed. It is signposted as the Balcón del Adarve. By its side you will find a quarter of old houses, whitewashed in narrow streets with flowers and decorative ironwork, which can match the Albaicín for its charm if not its size, proof that these little barrios are not confined to large, tourist cities. From the Plaza del Andalucia in the centre of town there is a signpost to the Fuente del Rey, a rather splendid fountain in a small park, reached by a street of rich Renaissance mansions.

Lunch in Priego de Córdoba.

The C336 now moves west, further escaping the cooling winds of the Sierra Nevada and bringing us closer to the hottest part of Spain, the boiling valley which lies between Córdoba and Seville. We pass through Cabra and on to Monturque where we join the main N331 from Málaga heading north.

Montilla

There is one more stop which may appeal to the visitor interested in Spanish food and wine, and a clue to it appears in the countryside, where the fields are gradually shifting from olive groves to vineyards. This is the region of Montilla-Moriles, home of the montilla wine which is famous throughout Spain and hardly known outside. Montilla is just off the road, a rather docile town with that air of seriousness which so often sits on those places which earn their living from the grape. Several of the *bodegas* welcome visitors during normal business hours.

In the Plaza de la Rosa, you will find a handful of dignified bars where quiet men sip their chosen drink over plates of tapas. Montilla, as anyone here will tell you, is the perfect aperitif and may be drunk as a white wine throughout a meal. If you ask for a *fino* around Córdoba, you will not receive a dry sherry, such as *La Ina*, but a dry montilla. It is an interesting drink, clearly related to sherry yet with a special, earthy character of its own, and certainly more sophisticated than most of the table wines produced in the south.

Córdoba

Córdoba is now a mere 25 miles away, and in a few minutes can be seen in the valley of the great Guadalquivir, the historic river which rises in the Sierra de Cazorla, then flows through Seville and on to the sea near Jerez. The entrance to the city is no more impressive than our arrival at Granada, though the traffic will normally be a little less horrendous. Depending on your choice of hotel, you must make a quick decision as you cross the bridge over the river – do you follow the signs which point to the Mezquita or go on towards the centre of town? The hotels which are placed within the old Jewish quarter, the Judería, are best reached by the Mezquita route, which turns right at this bridge and then left into the old quarter. There is a large car park marked at the entrance; you would be wise to park here if your hotel does not have a car park of its own. The Melia and the Parador lie ahead, well signposted, and you will also find parking spaces on the side road which runs along the main road after the Melia. Once you have found a car space in Córdoba, leave your vehicle there until you depart, since this is not a city built for the motor car.

Using this itinerary, you should arrive in Córdoba around late afternoon, which is probably too late to start serious sightseeing. A better idea is to explore the narrow alleys of the Judería which lead down to the great mosque, to lose your way in this warren of blind alleys and make chance finds of interesting buildings and sights such as the ornate patios, with their pottery and flowers, of which the city is so proud. Córdoba is a town of great life. The sounds of lively conversation, dancing and song flit around the Judería day and night and offer as many pleasures as the monuments we shall see tomorrow.

Overnight in Córdoba.

ACCOMMODATION

Córdoba attracts groups of coach tourists throughout the year, making booking essential. Hotel car parking is normally charged as a small additional sum per night.

Parador de la Arruzafa
Ctra. de El Brillante
Córdoba
Tel: 275900

This modern parador is exceedingly comfortable and has fine grounds. Its situation, two miles from the city, is something of a disadvantage, but does guarantee quiet nights.

Open all year
Rooms: 83
Facilities: outdoor pool, tennis
Credit cards: American Express, Diner's Club, Eurocard, Visa
Rating ****

Adarve
Magistral Gónzalez Francés 15
Córdoba
Tel: 481102

Luxurious hotel in an old mansion next to the Mezquita, the best place to stay in the Judería. Underground car parking.

Open all year
Rooms: 103
Credit cards: American Express, Diner's Club, Eurocard, Visa
Rating ****

Maimonides
Torrijos 4
Córdoba
Tel: 471500

Popular coach party hotel by the Mezquita, comfortable if lacking in character. Underground car parking.

Open all year
Rooms: 61
Credit cards: American Express, Diner's Club, Eurocard, Visa
Rating ***

El Triunfo
Cardenal González 79
Córdoba
Tel: 475500

Reasonably priced, comfortable rooms, close to the Triunfo column.

Open all year
Rooms: 47
Credit cards: American Express, Diner's Club, Eurocard, Visa
Rating ***

Melia Córdoba
Jardines de la Victoria
Córdoba
Tel: 298066

Large modern hotel at the edge of the Judería. Avoid the last two weeks of May when it is surrounded by a noisy, all-night fair.

Open all year
Rooms: 105
Facilities: outdoor pool, terrace with flowers
Credit cards: American Express, Diner's Club, Eurocard, Visa
Rating ****

El Califa
Lope de Hoces 14
Córdoba
Tel: 299400

Business hotel which can normally find rooms when others cannot. Near the Melia, and somewhat noisy in roadside rooms.

Open all year
Rooms: 46
Credit cards: Visa
Rating ***

EATING OUT

Córdoba is the home of one of the finest restaurants in Spain, the Caballo Rojo, which specialises in 'Mozarabic' cuisine, dishes influenced by the city's Moslem past. Expect meat and game with fruit. Other local specialities include *alcochofas montana*, artichokes in a cream sauce, *rabas de toro*, an oxtail stew, and *salmorejo*, a delicious variation on gazpacho which includes white bread and an abundance of tomatoes.

El Caballo Rojo
Cardenal Herrero 28
Córdoba
Tel: 474342

No food lover can leave Córdoba without visiting the Caballo Rojo which is renowned throughout Spain. Prices are now expensive but there is a reasonable menu of the day which includes two specialities, *alcochofas montana* and *rabas de toro*. The ambience is one of upper class Spanish gentility, the menu an intriguing mix of traditional cuisine and reinvented dishes designed to reflect the city's Moslem history.

Open all year, seven days a week
Credit cards: American Express, Diner's Club, Eurocard, Visa
Rating ****

El Churrasco
Romero 16
Córdoba
Tel: 290819

In some ways more memorable than the Caballo Rojo, this is an atmospheric old house in the Judería with a busy local following and a charcoal grill, serving meat and fish from counter cabinets. Pretty patio with charcoal braziers under the table to warm diners in winter. Specialities include *churrasco*, grilled pork with a selection of piquant sauces, and the best *salmorejo* in town. Excellent house Rioja and bar service for budget diners.

Closed Thursdays and the whole of August
Credit cards: American Express, Diner's Club, Eurocard, Visa
Rating ***

Bar-Restaurante Federación de Peñas
Conde y Luque 8
Córdoba
Tel: 475427

The patio of a Judería mansion has been turned into a pleasant dining area by one of the city brotherhoods involved in social work. The menu is mainly fixed price set meals of standard dishes, all reasonably priced and well cooked, much better than one will find in the standard restaurant.

Open every day
No credit cards
Rating **

Córdoba, and the Judería in particular, has many small bars serving tapas and quick meals. The Taberna del Potro, in the Plaza del Potro, is such a place; the *pollo ajillo*, chicken in garlic sauce is pure Spanish home cooking.

CORDOBA: USEFUL INFORMATION	
Tourist office:	Plaza de Judá Leví
	Tel: 290740
Population:	284,737

Córdoba Cathedral

DAY 6

Córdoba, the Great Mosque, the Judería and the Alcázar Real, on foot.

The greatest sight in Córdoba is the Mezquita, a sumptuous mosque and cathedral combined. The day begins with a view of the city from the south bank of the Guadalquivir at the Tower of the Calahorra, then moves to the Mezquita, the old Jewish quarter of the Judería, and finally the fortress of the Alcázar Real.

Overnight in Córdoba.

Map reference
Córdoba   37°52′N 4°45′W

Breakfast in Córdoba.

From the south bank of the Guadalquivir, the tower of the Calahorra provides the visitor with a panorama of the ancient city opposite, with its wide mix of architectural styles and periods. From here, one can easily walk to the mosque and cathedral, the Mezquita, visit the important buildings of the Jewish quarter, the Judería, and, finally, the fortress built for the Christian monarchs after the Reconquest, the Alcázar Real.

The best place to begin a tour of Córdoba is on the far side of the Guadalquivir. Cross by the Puente Romano, the original Roman bridge, behind the Mezquita, then enter the tower of the Calahorra which stands on the south bank by the bridge. From its ramparts, there is a view of the old city which will help you find your way around over the next few hours.

In front, at the end of the bridge sits a Renaissance arch and, beside it, the column of El Triunfo. Behind lies the rather puzzling mass of the Mezquita itself, hiding the Judería which runs as a warren of streets, alleys and dead-ends beyond. To the left are the walls of the Alcázar Real. You may feel that the Renaissance arch and the frankly hideous Triunfo column look a little out of place, and you would not be alone.

Yet Córdoba is nothing if not a confluence of centuries, however inharmonious this may seem at times. Roman columns rub cheek by jowl with Renaissance doorways, Arabic horseshoe arches support baroque ceilings. All is fused into one, occasionally with difficulty, and each successive generation has borrowed, literally, from the previous to build its creations. Córdoba is the only place I know where at least one Roman capital now serves to support the brickwork of a garage. Before leaving the ramparts, you should note the remains of watermills in the river, and the odd grazing cow on the grass growing in the Guadalquivir silt.

The Calahorra is more than a viewing platform for this odd panorama of the city. It has also been furnished with an ultra-modern system of tape-recorded tableaux which attempt to explain a little of the city's history in several different languages. You rent your headset at the entrance then push buttons in each room to activate the recorded program as a series of lights illuminate the displays. This is by no means as uninteresting as it may sound, though some may find the opening chamber a little puzzling.

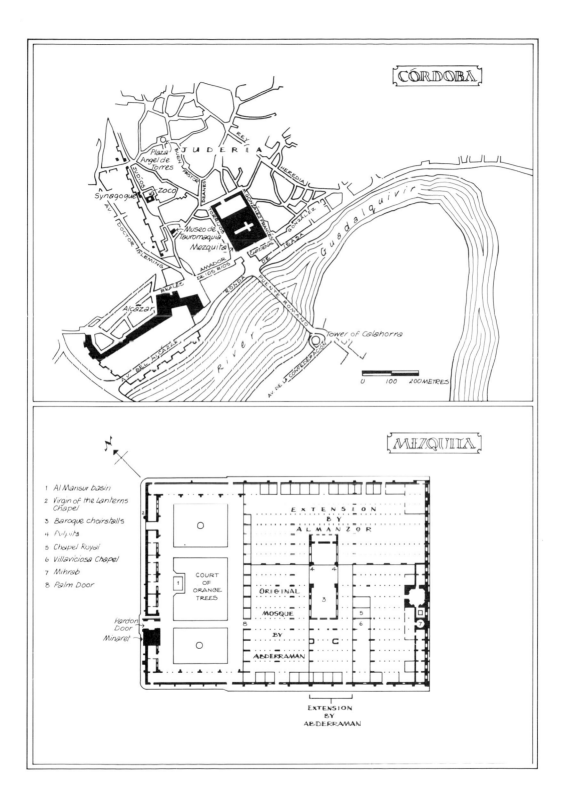

CÓRDOBA

JUDERIA
Plaza
Angel de
Torres
Synagogue
Zoco
Museo de
Tauromaquia
Mezquita
Alcázar
Guadalquivir
Tower of Calahorra
River

0   100   200 METRES

MEZQUITA

1 Al Mansur basin
2 Virgin of the Lanterns
   Chapel
3 Baroque choirstalls
4 Pulpits
5 Chapel Royal
6 Villaviciosa Chapel
7 Mihrab
8 Palm Door

Pardon
Door
Minaret

COURT
OF
ORANGE
TREES

EXTENSION
BY
ALMANZOR

ORIGINAL
MOSQUE
BY
ABDERRAMAN

EXTENSION
BY
ABDERRAMAN

It features four famous figures connected with the city, the philosophers Averroes, Maimonides and Ibn Arabi, and the 13th-century monarch Alfonso X in conversation about Islam and Christianity. The sentiments are somewhat utopian and the portrait of Alfonso as a king who might have forged a new idealistic Spain of free Moslems, Christians and Jews is debatable to say the least. But one does comprehend the importance which Córdoba held in the Mediterranean world of long ago. In its day, and that ran between the 8th and 13th centuries, it was the greatest city of learning in Europe, the home of vast libraries which attracted the attention of scholars of all religions.

It is this which sets Córdoba apart from Granada. The latter was a city created by a Moslem world in exile and under threat for its very existence. For more than two centuries before Granada fell, its rulers were little more than puppets of Christian kings. Córdoba, on the other hand, was the earlier creation of an expanding and vibrant Moslem empire which looked to extend the rule of Allah further into Europe with Córdoba as its capital city, much as Baghdad ruled the east. The beauty of this civilised city astonished all who witnessed it, leading Alfonso to order that he be buried there, a wish that went unfulfilled. An impressive miniature reconstruction of the Mezquita at its Islamic height gives us a hint of what Alfonso saw. Only the Romans are absent from this brief offering on the history of Córdoba, and evidence of their presence in what was a regional capital of the empire is still everywhere. Seneca was born in the city and is commemorated in the names of bookshops throughout Andalucia to this day.

Returning over the Puente Romano it becomes apparent that our misgivings about the arch and the Triunfo column were correct. As you cross the road, there is a plaque with a poem by the famous native poet Luis de Gongora, in which he describes the city as a 'flower of Spain'; clearly a man who knew how to avert his eyes in the correct places.

We are then faced with the Mezquita, or rather its outside wall, a *mélange* of styles and influences. A stroll around the outside will convince you of the varied origins of this structure. Scarcely a century seems to have backed away from the opportunity to 'improve' some part of it, yet very early work, dating back to the 10th century, does survive.

At the northern, townside, corner, you will even find an exterior chapel containing a rather doleful 20th-century portrait of the Virgin by the Córdoban painter Julio Romero de Torres. Torres was better known for his portraits of Córdoban prostitutes and seems well off the mark here. It is intriguing that he was commissioned to produce such a painting even after causing a scandal with the frankness of his earlier work. Perhaps we should bear in mind the words of Ibn Arabi in the Calahorra who spoke of physical love being an expression of the divine, an idea which runs as a philosophical thread from the Arab thinkers into Christian beliefs in Andalucia.

The true entrance to the Mezquita is the Puerta del Pardon, part of the belltower formed from the original minaret. At the time of writing this has been closed and visitors must make their way in by the less interesting Puerta del Casa Gordo, next to Sr Torres' sad-eyed Virgin. We find ourselves in the Patio de los Naranjos, originally the area where the Moslem faithful would perform their ritual ablutions before entering the holy area of the mosque. It is worth returning to examine the Puerta del Pardon from inside the patio, since there is extensive stucco work to be seen and you can easily avert your gaze from a hideous Renaissance ceiling. Steps by the side lead into the tower, the interior of which is the original Moslem creation, and it provides views of the city.

Once more the Mezquita authorities have barred an original entrance and forced us to take a more awkward route than visitors of only a decade ago. The true entrance to the cathedral is via the Puerta de las Palmas, opposite the Puerta del Pardon. It is easily recognisable from the Roman columns, complete with inscriptions, which stand outside it. Today we must move to the left and buy our tickets at the northern end which immediately leads us into the most recent, and unsatisfactory part of the mosque, the extension ordered by Almansor.

But the new visitor will hardly notice this as he enters the building, for there remains nothing in the world like the first view of the Mezquita and the astonishing discovery that, within this odd facade, there lurks a magical forest of pillars and striped horseshoe arches which stretch in every direction to no apparent plan.

At this point the visitor may throw guide books to the wind and choose to wander around in sheer astonishment, a reaction with which it is difficult to argue. If you wish to see this building in some kind of historical perspective, however, you may do so like this...

Ignoring the parties of tourists and the curious realisation that, within the centre of this Moslem feast there appears to be a complete baroque cathedral, walk to your right, following the wall. As you progress the floor will dip, taking you into the very first part of the mosque, that of Abderrahman I which dates from the late 8th century.

This being Córdoba, there was a substantial amount of building material ready to hand, including the Visigothic church of Saint Vincent which stood on the spot at the time and had itself been created out of the previous occupant, a Roman temple. A remnant of this process is the landmark which marks the starting point of our tour, a simple Visigothic font with a rectangular basin which stands not far from the Mezquita wall. Its simple carvings are reminiscent of work from more northern climes, a characteristic of much Visigothic art.

Standing at the ancient font, we may now begin to look more closely at the immediate surroundings. It becomes apparent, first of all, that the initial symmetry of this part of the structure is misleading. The columns and capitals vary enormously in width, style, material and height, and range from Roman and Visigothic sources to the occasional Arabic original. Around the periphery of the building are a series of enclosed chambers, small chapels containing little of interest to the non-specialist, while the occasional Renaissance painting finds its way onto the central floor of the mosque. It is tempting to believe that this arrangement represents the norm throughout the whole of the Mezquita, yet, as we shall see, the building is far more complex than it might appear at first glance.

After examining some of the columns in this ancient part of the building, move to the left and walk through the central Renaissance walkway, behind the rear of the choir of the cathedral. We pass through a horseshoe arch of purely Christian origins and approach a portion of the far wall which draws visitors like bees to honey. Pause for a moment, however, and notice the two fine Roman alabaster columns close by, spiralled most beautifully. And inside the closed chamber which stands to our left, the Capilla Real, it is possible to see the most ornate stucco work carried out by *mudéjar* craftsmen. The central section of the mosque, from behind the choir to the rear, was the work of Abderrahman's son.

The section ahead dates from a century later, under Alhaken II, and here you can see a distinct progression in styles. The arches become more elaborate and there is a new intricacy to the capitals and columns. The focal point is the glorious mihrab around which visitors always cluster. This was the holiest point of the mosque, a small, intimate chamber set into the mosque wall and reserved for the most important ceremonies. The central horseshoe entrance arch is adorned with a mosaic of many colours which give it the appearance of being bejewelled, and the whole is beautifully lit. The mihrab itself may not be entered but it is possible to see the fine decorative work, in gypsum plaster, on the ceiling. The function of the two subsidiary arches is unknown. This brightly coloured holy place and the forest of columns are the two most abiding memories of the Mezquita.

The rest of the cathedral – for the whole of the building is consecrated as such – is less interesting. Returning to the centre, what we will, inevitably, think of as the cathedral proper is a fairly predictable baroque creation which pales in interest against that which encloses it. There is a finely carved choir, which may be examined closely, and little else to excite interest. Next to the mihrab is the cathedral treasury which displays the array of processional gilt and silver one must expect in Spanish cathedrals; many of the vessels claim to contain saintly relics. The tour guides will wax lyrical about its value and beauty but, deprived of their opinions, the independent traveller may come to the individual conclusion that much of the work is frankly vulgar. The tone of the sacristy may be judged from the canvas found on the left as you enter. This depicts a victorious Ferdinand III accepting the surrender of the city which is seen behind the Christian hero. Miraculously, the Mezquita has already been transformed into the cathedral architecture which we see today.

The remaining portion of the Mezquita is the addition of Almanzor, which is where we entered the building. This destroyed the symmetry of the mosque, in which the mihrab was placed centrally at the far end of the building from the door where worshippers entered, and was built more to make a political point for the ruling dynasty than to improve the mosque. The work seems simpler and more perfunctory than the varied columns and arch arrangements seen earlier, which is why I urge the visitor to work his way around the mosque in the direction outlined above.

The logical place to visit after the Mezquita is the Alcázar Real, the Christian fortress found by turning right at the Triunfo, after the tourist office. Sadly, the tourist authorities have decided to thwart us in this simple desire, since they close the Alcázar between 1.30 and 5pm each day. Of all the siestas in Andalucia, this is the least excusable, since the Alcázar contains gardens which would offer a relaxing way to doze away a quiet afternoon. Indeed the place is open at night during the summer, from 10pm to midnight, for nothing but pleasant strolling, and very popular with the locals it is too. Nevertheless, if we have followed our instincts and visited the Torre de la Calahorra and the Mezquita there will now be insufficient time to take in the Alcázar before the doors close.

Lunch at the Caballo Rojo or, for less formality, the bar of El Churrasco.

This is the time to explore the Judería in some detail, since many of its pleasures do not rely on the whims of tourist officials and, when they do, at least see fit to reopen at 4pm. A detailed itinerary around this charming warren of narrow streets and patios is by no means impossible but you will not find it here since, as I have said, serendipity is part of the area's attraction. It is sufficient to list the sights which you may wish to seek out on your explorations.

The Synagogue is the last of its age remaining in Spain, all others being destroyed during the foolish expulsion of the Jews by Ferdinand and Isabel after the conquest of Granada. Humane considerations apart, this act deprived the nation of a community well versed in business expertise and set the fanatical tone which was to turn into the Grand Inquisition. There is little to see in the tiny building, as the small entrance fee reflects, yet the modesty of its charm is impressive in itself after the grandeur of the great mosque. It is ironic that the Jews found themselves better treated by the Moslem caliphs than the Christian kings who succeeded them.

The Judería also includes the Museo de Tauromaquia, a collection of items concerning bullfighting which will baffle the uninitiated. The city's bullfighting hero is Manolete whose photograph still adorns many bars and restaurants more than 40 years after he died in the ring. The Zoco is a small Arab market – souk – which has been restored to attract the attention of the passing tourist with gifts, a café and occasional displays of dancing. The structure is not without interest, unlike its contents.

A word is required on that Córdoban speciality the patio. It will come as no surprise to the reader that here we have, once more, a relic of the Arab centuries, since there was nothing the Moslem liked more in his home than a spacious patio, with water and plants behind the rather bare walls which enclosed his mansion. So today the Córdoban cultivates his patio, decorating it with tiles, erecting fountains, and trailing geraniums down the iron grills and over large pots. This is a cult which culminates each year, at the beginning of May, in a two-week festival of patios at the end of which prizes are awarded for the most sumptuous displays. They are much coveted, and the winners will proudly announce their successes in posters at the corner of the street in order to lead the passer-by to the patio in question.

Peering inside the front door of a house in Córdoba is, then, more a compliment than an intrusion, and it may be difficult to keep a proud owner out of a photograph of a winning entry.

By now the guards of the Alcázar Real may have awoken after their lunch. There is a handsome view from the battlements, a famous Roman sarcophagus and spacious gardens laid out in the Arab manner, though the standard of care is nothing compared to that lavished on the Generalife.

The Alcázar began its career as a royal palace and was later used as a prison during the Inquisition, a purpose to which it was well suited as the visitor, seeing the substantial walls, will appreciate. The Alcázar is of minor architectural interest compared with the Mezquita, but it is a most pleasant place to while away an hour, or an evening, in the company of chattering Córdoban families who enter for free and treat it as a municipal park.

Overnight in Córdoba.

Accommodation and restaurants, see pp. 76-9.

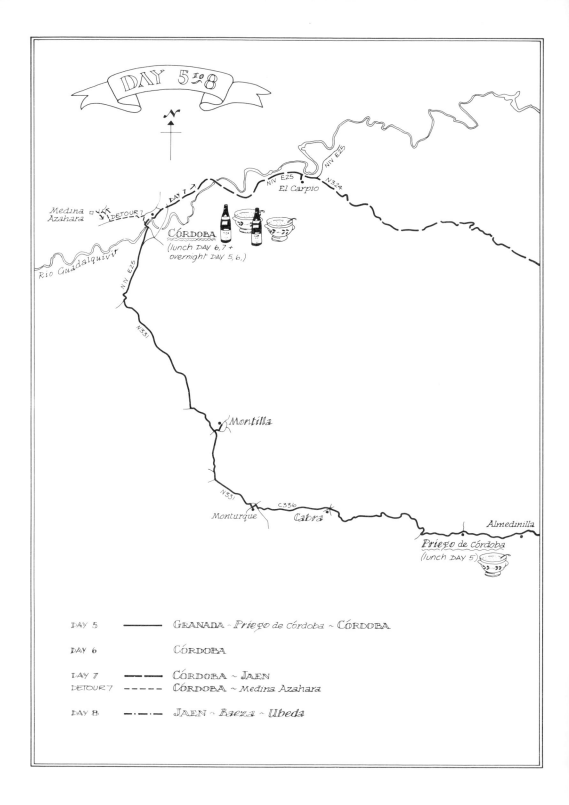

DAY 5 to 8

Medina Azahara □ DETOUR 7
DAY 7
El Carpio
N IV E25
N IV E25
N 324

CÓRDOBA
(lunch DAY 6,7 +
overnight DAY 5,6,)

Rio Guadalquivir

N IV E25

N 331

Montilla

N 331

Monturque   C336   Cabra

Almedinilla

Priego de Córdoba
(lunch DAY 5)

DAY 5	————	GRANADA ~ *Priego de Córdoba* ~ CÓRDOBA
DAY 6		CÓRDOBA
DAY 7	– – –	CÓRDOBA ~ JAEN
DETOUR 7	- - - - -	CÓRDOBA ~ *Medina Azahara*
DAY 8	–·–·–	JAEN ~ *Baeza* ~ *Ubeda*

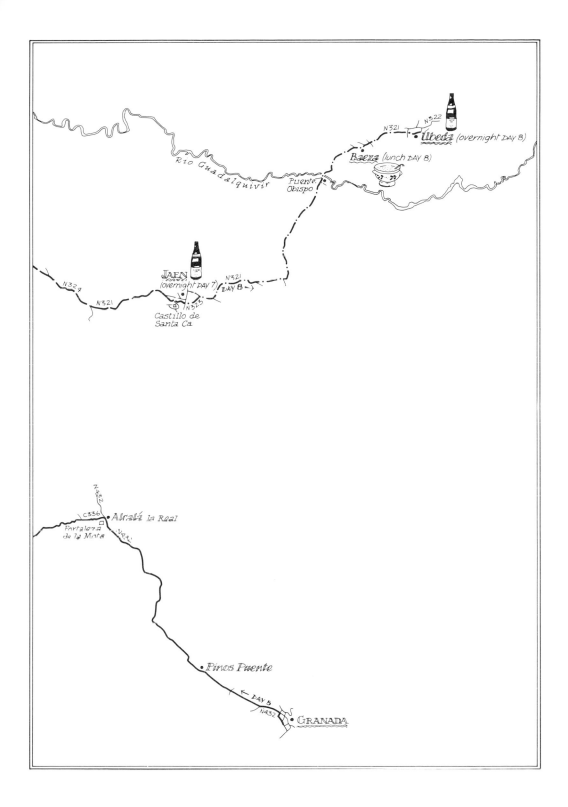

Río Guadalquivir

N321 N322

Úbeda (overnight DAY 8)

Baeza (lunch DAY 8)

Puente Obispo

JAEN (overnight DAY 7)

N321 DAY 8

N324 N321

N325

Castillo de Santa Ca

C336

Alcalá la Real

Fortaleza de la Mota

Pinos Puente

DAY 5

N432

GRANADA

Jaen

DAY 7

Córdoba to Jaen, about 60 miles.

The morning allows time to visit the magnificent Archeological Museum of Córdoba which has a rich collection of Roman, Visigothic and Moslem artefacts. Close by are the Plaza del Potro, Museo des Bellas Artes and the Museo de Julio Romero de Torres, dedicated to the local painter. The remains of the Moslem town of Medina Azahara can easily be seen before leaving Córdoba. The journey continues through olive-growing country to Jaen where there is a spectacular parador in a castle overlooking the city.

Overnight in Jaen.

Route shown p. 90.

Map references
Córdoba	37° 52´N 4° 45´W
El Carpio	37° 58´N 4° 30´W
Jaen	37° 48´N 3° 45´W

Breakfast in Córdoba.

The Archeological Museum of Córdoba is the most delightful of its kind in southern Spain. It may be found in a Renaissance palace, the Palacio de los Paez, to the north of the Mezquita, signposted from the busy street of Rey Heredia. The imposing 16th-century building stands in a small square containing fragments of Roman masonry, an odd introduction to a museum which is otherwise impeccably ordered.

You enter through a lovely patio similarly decked in Roman stone objects, but there are signs of order. Bougainvillea trails down one wall, lemon and ivy another. To the right is a small hall of rather dull paleolithic objects, though there is a plaque above the door dedicated to the Caudillo Franco dating from 1965; not many of *those* have survived the post-Falange rewriting of street names and signs.

There is a collection of pre-Roman Iberian work, then an extension of the patio where beautifully restored Roman mosaics decorate the walls. The centrepiece is a well-known statue of Mithras killing the bull, a snake biting the animal and a dog licking the blood from its wound. A curious and cryptic feature is a scorpion attached to the bull's penis.

Less opaque is a third-century Christian sarcophagus depicting, in relief panels separated by spiral columns, scenes from the old and new testaments. Adam and Eve are clearly seen wearing fig leaves, with the serpent between them and a few apples still remaining on the tree. Elsewhere are several well-preserved Roman coffins and a series of headstones which the Latin reader will quickly translate from the clear script.

Visigothic artefacts fill a complete room and once more remind the northern visitor of Saxon and Celtic work in their simple, elegant depiction of crosses. A brief glance at the legends to the exhibits in the museum reveals that many of them were uncovered in the very heart of the city, often during building work in the busiest of streets.

The first floor is reached by a broad staircase along which are positioned several superb colourful Roman mosaics. Here we find a vast collection of Moslem work: everyday pottery, the iron braziers used for heating which one will still find in restaurants like El Churrasco in winter today, and decorative ceramic work which is now copied by the city's modern potters for sale, at a price, to appreciative visitors. There is an acclaimed, stylised bronze and enamel stag found at Medina Azahara and another reconstruction of the Mezquita.

From the museum, cross the square outside and head downhill until reaching the busy road of San Fernando which leads to the river. Here, along Calle Lucano, you will find signs to the Plaza del Potro, a delightful little square with a fountain at its centre. There are three buildings of interest here. The first is the Posada del Potro, a former inn built around a courtyard which will remind the English visitor of similar buildings from Elizabethan times, such as the George at Southwark. Cervantes mentions the plaza in *Don Quixote* and it is claimed that he lodged at the Posada. On the other side of the square we find two very different art galleries. One is the city Museo des Bellas Artes, housed in a 15th-century building, which can claim canvases by Goya and a wide selection of work by Córdoban artists up to modern times. It is no more satisfying as a whole than that in the palace at Granada, living, like all Andalucian galleries, under the shadow of the two great collections of the region, those of Seville and Cádiz, but it merits some time.

The collection next to it, in the Museo de Julio Romero de Torres, is a curiosity more of interest for local colour than artistic merit. We have already seen one of Torres' less satisfying works in the exterior chapel of the Mezquita. Here you will find the paintings for which he is better known, a series of sensual depictions of the women as dark-skinned beauties, eyes burning with passion.

His paintings of the city prostitutes provoked an outcry in the 1920s. This was because of their sexual content, not the sanitised and romantic picture they paint of what was then and remains a squalid and impoverished calling. One need only take a wrong turning in a large city such as Córdoba or Granada today to discover that the subject matter of Torres' 'ladies of the night' are far removed from the glamorous, sultry figures we see on canvas, and there is no reason to suppose matters were different sixty years ago.

Torres' work is fascinating because it points up the conflicts in Andalucian society between sensuality and a fervent religious temperament, though it may be that this is a contradiction which exists only for those who come from outside Spain.

A little further along from the Plaza del Potro, past the excellent Taberna del Potro on the continuation of Calle Lucano, you will find a montilla *bodega*, Campo, housed in a charming old mansion. The language barrier may prevent much information of any use being shared here, but the warmth of the welcome translates into any language and the barrels and small patios which make up the *bodega* are undeniably picturesque.

There are many other, minor sights in Córdoba which are best appreciated on a second visit, for it is easy to fall into an overwhelming round of museum and church going. A small foretaste of what else lies here can be seen on our return to the Judería. At the busy street of San Fernando walk a little away from the river, turning through an arch. Soon, to our left, is a street called Cabezas, a curious name since it simply means 'Heads'. An explanation may be found on a plaque on one of the many fine mansions in the street. This relates that in the year 974 the heads of the seven sons of a Christian lord were displayed on the house, part of an internecine feud. Should the onlooker be doubtful, the plaque backs this claim with the information that it is attested to by two historians, Aben Hayan and Ambrosio de Morales, and a Castilian ballad singer. Visiting the museum and art galleries may well occupy a full morning.

Detour

You may be feeling full of Moslem architecture by now, but there is one more example which should be considered. This is a visit to the ruins of Medina Azahara which lie six miles out of the city, signposted along the street named after the monument which branches from the Avenida Argentina, the broad carriageway containing a park which is a continuation of the road from the Guadalquivir bridge. This is an oddly atmospheric place, the remains of a complete Moslem city which was sacked and destroyed only a century after its creation by a rival Moslem faction. Medina Azahara has been plundered over the years to provide masonry for work in Córdoba, but now there is much careful restoration work taking place and one begins to appreciate the splendour which this city must have possessed during its brief existence. The doors close for the afternoon at 2pm – 1.30pm on Sundays – just around the time that most visitors might like to arrive.

Lunch at Córdoba.

After lunch, it is time to move on – and it is advisable to eat before leaving, since there are few facilities *en route*. The journey to Jaen is an easy one which can be accommodated quite adequately by a late afternoon start. We leave Córdoba by the main road to Madrid, the NIV which takes us past the Mezquita along the banks of the Guadalquivir. Passing through a procession of dull flat suburbs one comes to realise that this is a city of some size, much larger than the compact quarter of the Judería would lead you to believe. In spite of appearances, Córdoba is actually larger than Granada by some 40,000 people.

The NIV is a fast and adequate road. Were one to be so minded, a swift drive would bring one to Madrid in around four hours from here. After El Carpio, we turn right onto the N324 signposted for Jaen – pronounced 'Chine', with the 'ch' as in 'loch'. This takes us away from a line of industrial estates into rich agricultural land.

It is a pleasant drive, past olive groves and colourful banks of varied wild flowers which thrive beyond the reach of herbicides, a sight one has forgotten in many parts of Europe. Frequently there is an earthy smell in the air; it is that of olive pressings. Mounds of black, dry husks can be seen by the side of the road.

Jaen

Approaching Jaen, the outline of the great fortress high above the town appears on the horizon. This is the Castillo de Santa Catalina, a monument which has been turned into a splendid parador. Whether you stay here for the night or not – and I urge that you do – your first act on reaching the town should be to visit the castle, which is found at the top of a winding road marked as you enter (you must ignore the sign trying to entice you into the centre of the city first). The castle itself is rather plain, and the parador portion has been restored twice in its history, once very recently.

A footpath leads beyond the castle to a large cross at the end of the peak, and from here there is a panorama of the city and the surrounding region. The tiled roofs of the oldest quarter are exceptionally attractive as is the cathedral, with its immense classical front. We have finally found a post-Moslem building of some size of which no part demands that the discriminating avert their eyes. There will be no time for sights, and beyond the cathedral there is little else for the casual visitor to enjoy. A walk around the narrow streets surrounding the cathedral, which seem tiny by comparison with its enormous bulk, is as much as you can hope to achieve before returning to the parador and enjoying a decent meal and a night which will be blessed with something rarely to be found in Córdoba or Granada – total silence.

Overnight in Jaen.

ACCOMMODATION

Parador de Santa Catalina
Jaen
Tel: 264411

A unique and memorable parador, the Castillo is undoubtedly the best place to stay in Jaen, and advance booking is therefore essential. There is an excellent dining room serving a moderately innovative menu of local dishes.

Open all year
Credit cards: American Express, Diner's Club, Eurocard, Visa
Rooms: 43
Rating ****

Condestable Iranzo
Paseo de la Estación 32
Jaen
Tel: 222800

Comfortable business hotel close to the town centre, reasonably priced for the standard of facility it offers.

Open all year
Credit cards: Visa
Rooms: 147
Rating ***

EATING OUT

Jaen is not known for its gastronomic wonders. The dining room of the parador is the best bet for the visitor who does not wish to eat in the town. At the time of writing, some restoration work is being undertaken so it is impossible to predict whether the parador dining room will retain its previous ambience, which was that of a set from the film of *El Cid*, complete with armour and tournament banners. Two restaurants deserve mention in the town centre.

Jockey Club
Paseo de la Estación 20
Jaen
Tel: 251018

Standard upmarket Spanish cooking in pleasant surroundings – one of several establishments in Jaen which bear English names for long-forgotten reasons.

Open every day
Credit cards: American Express, Diner's Club, Eurocard, Visa
Rating ***

99

Granada

Los Mariscos
Nueva 2
Tel: 253206
Jaen

Surprisingly good fish and shellfish for an inland town, close to the centre.

Open every day
Credit cards: Visa
Rating ***

JAEN: USEFUL INFORMATION
Tourist office: Avda. de Madrid, 10-A
                      Tel: 222737
Population: 96,429
Facilities: bullring

DAY 8

Jaen to Ubeda via Baeza, around 40 miles.

There is a visit to Jaen's impressive cathedral. Then the route winds
through olive groves to two little-known towns, Baeza and Ubeda, containing a wealth of Renaissance architecture. This is the northernmost part of
the journey, at the very periphery of Andalucia.

Overnight at Ubeda.

Route shown p. 90.

Map references

Jaen	37° 48´N 3° 45´W
Baeza	37° 59´N 3° 28´W
Ubeda	38° 04´N 3·22´W

Breakfast at Jaen.

The Castle and parador apart, the great cathedral is the principal sight in Jaen, literally since some element of it seems visible from any viewpoint in the centre of the old quarter. Jaen has many items of religious interest to the Spanish Catholic beyond the cathedral, which itself owns a handkerchief of St Veronica bearing an image reputed to be that of Christ, pressed upon it when the saint wiped the face of Jesus. It is kept secure throughout the week except for Fridays when it is on view between 11am and 5pm. This is not the place to argue the case against accepting the truth of such relics – there is, for example, little evidence that St Veronica ever existed. The belief in these icons is so strong that it, in truth, is more impressive than the objects themselves.

The round of religious sights is one which I do not intend to detail here, for I feel it will be of little use to the casual visitor for whom the city's chief interest is a secular admiration of the cathedral. As we have already discovered from the heights of Santa Catalina, it is of a well-balanced design and shows nothing of the excesses which may be found in other post-Moslem buildings we have encountered.

There is an argument that the massive structure is too large for the web of tiny streets which surrounds it, and it is true that one would normally expect a structure of this size to have a more substantial, open approach. The architect, Andres de Vandelvira, may have thought so himself, but his commission was for the cathedral, not its environs. One practical note of caution is required, however. It is extremely difficult to park close to the cathedral because of these narrow streets, and I would personally rather walk a half mile to the cathedral than attempt to find space for a car in these sadly congested alleyways. My advice would be to do the same, or even take a taxi from the parador into the town or back.

Inside the cathedral there is a fine wooden choir – the *coro* – often a reliable feature in the most tasteless of Andalucian cathedrals, as we have discovered in Málaga and Córdoba. The cathedral museum contains work by Ribera and a head of John the Baptist by one Valdés Leal, a curious fellow of the Sevillian school who was the creator of what is, in my opinion, the most chilling painting to be found in Andalucia, a grisly canvas warning of the inevitability of death which may be found in a home for the elderly in

Seville, the Hospital de la Caridad. In the cathedral, you will also find two candlesticks by the craftsman who created the famous *reja* screen in the Capilla Real at Granada, Master Bartolomé who was a native of Jaen.

As you may have gathered, commissions in architecture and church art in this period were not shared out among many; the same names crop up throughout the whole of Andalucia, and experts are able to chart the development, or regression, of individual artists from church to church.

To leave Jaen, find the main road to Granada and head south. After a few minutes, follow the signs to Ubeda and Albacete on the N321. The road quickly rises into somewhat bare high ground, once again dominated by olive production, and there is not the slightest sign that two of the most delightful towns of southern Spain lie but a few miles ahead.

Baeza

We cross the Guadalquivir once more at Puente Obispo – the Archbishop's bridge – and you can see the construction itself from a newer bridge, the arches diminishing in size to adapt to the difference in height between the banks; an unusual sight indeed. Then soon we see on the horizon the town of Baeza. On entering, look for the signs which point to the Plaza del Populo and the tourist information office, in a small Renaissance square with a fountain of rather battered lions to the right, then park and plunder the well-stocked tourist department for whatever additional information on the region you require.

Lunch in Baeza.

Baeza is a foretaste of what we shall see in full splendour less than six miles away in Ubeda: a true Renaissance town largely untouched by the ravages of modern development. The historical centres of both Baeza and Ubeda are small enough for you to find your way around with the aid of the maps here, so I do not intend to describe individual walking itineraries. Instead, I shall outline the most important sights of each and allow you to find your own way around; this approach might not work in Granada's Albaicín, but I feel it is most appropriate with these small, homogenous communities.

103

In Baeza you face two choices. Either you may leave the car where it is near the Plaza del Pópulo or drive around, underneath the city walls following the sign for the Paseo de los Murallas and park near a large grey cross from which there is access to the old quarter by the Calle de la Merced. The latter is picturesque and you will often disturb several specimens of that delightful species the vibrantly coloured hoopoe, which make their startled, dipping flight at your approach. It is, perhaps, a measure of Baeza's calm that these normally shy birds will make their home so close to man.

Before leaving the Plaza del Pópulo, examine the tourist office itself, for it is a fine Plateresque building, of the early 16th century. The tourist office confusingly adds that the first mass after its Reconquest in 1227 was said from the balcony, omitting to tell the puzzled visitor that the building incorporated part of an early chapel which was attached to the Jaen gateway. The elegant galleried Renaissance building in the same square is the original slaughterhouse of the town, surely one of the most lovely ex-abattoirs – it now houses the town archives – in existence. The fountain deserves to look a little battered, being Carthaginian in origin.

The Barrio Monumental contains a wealth of old buildings, many in the course of restoration. In the square which fronts the cathedral stands the Palace of Jabalquinto, a grand Gothic civil structure – that is one commissioned by the state, not the church – which will one day be abandoned by the workmen making it ready for the public once more. I am unable to enthuse about the cathedral, which is 16th century and rather grey and obese, though there is the mudéjar Puerta de la Luna to cheer one. Behind the cathedral lies an interesting tangle of alleys which lead to the outskirts of the town. The Cabrera House, in Calle San Pablo, is an outstanding Renaissance mansion built for a family of the local nobility. A detailed list of other fine palaces is available from the tourist office, though I would stress that there is more of this kind, and better, to come shortly.

Ubeda

And so to Ubeda, which we find further along the road to Albacete. The ramshackle industrial buildings which greet us below the hill of the town are simply signs of its new agricultural prosperity. Its Renaissance heart remains well hidden until we are in its midst. Follow the signs for the parador and cling to them doggedly as we rise over the crest of the hill then once more descend through a succession of narrow twists and turns past grand houses which demand a second glance. With little warning, there is a left turn into a lovely square and, facing us, a fine Plateresque church front with, to its left, the golden stone of a beautiful palace. The latter is the Parador del Condestable Dávalos, a historic monument in its own right and, to the delight of everyone who visits, one of the very best paradors in the whole of Spain.

Ubeda makes Baeza's promise real. The restoration process, where it was required, is largely complete, bringing us a real Renaissance town in all its glory. Columns, galleries, patios and mythical decorative work stare at us from every corner, yet there is no question of architectural indigestion. Ubeda was designed by many hands over the centuries but, in its old quarter, they each worked for the same end. It is rather as if we had wandered onto the set of a magnificent opera only to discover that the cast had disappeared leaving mere mortals to populate the magnificent streets.

Again, I shall not presume to hand out precise details of where you should roam, since that would be destroying much of the town's delight. Certain buildings should not be missed, however. The parador, with its admirable patio, is one and I shall offer gastronomic reasons later for why a visit is essential. The Chapel of El Salvador next to it, with the Plateresque facade, is another, though I suspect the interior will appeal only to high church specialists. The chapel is the work of the great Diego Siloé whose artistry may be seen throughout Andalucia.

Further along from the parador stands the Church of Santa Maria de los Reales Alcázares, which has a famous cloister and Plateresque work which reveals how little those of the last century knew about restoration. You may compare the pre-restoration material with the post yourself, since the perpetrators took the trouble to mark their work.

A little way behind the parador, in the Plaza del Primero de Mayo, there is the Church of San Pablo, a Renaissance building with a simpler, perhaps greater beauty than that expressed in Siloé's El Salvador (the latter was originally a private chapel for the palace of the Condestable and therefore more sumptuous). A corner of the same square also houses the Italianate Old Town Hall. The vast Santiago Hospital, some way out of the old barrio, the House of the Savages, with its curious wild men supporting a noble coat of arms, and the Casa de las Torres with its extraordinarily ornate facade all deserve to be seen. The list must end somewhere, and I have omitted to mention... but no, you must make some discoveries for yourself with the aid of the helpful tourist office which you will find in the Plaza del Ayuntamiento.

Leaving beautiful masonry aside, you should also remember that truly typical local pottery and craftwork made from esparto grass – you will see both used in the parador – can be found in the local quarter of the Calle de Valencia beyond the Puerta del Losal, set out for sale in the street where the ceramic ware is also dried.

Ubeda is by no means as unknown as it was even five years ago, and you may even see the odd coach party taking tea at the parador. Yet these old stones cry out for company in what was once, visibly, a great and grand Renaissance city and I cannot begrudge it new admirers.

Overnight in Ubeda.

ACCOMMODATION

Parador del Condestable Dávalos
Pl. Varquez de Molina 1
Ubeda
Tel: 750345

Quite simply one of the finest paradors in Spain. If you intend to stay in only one parador on your visit, this should be it. There is a beautiful patio, a fine restaurant, and the whole has been decorated in immaculate taste. Booking essential.

Open all year
Rooms: 26
Credit cards: American Express, Diner's Club, Eurocard, Visa
Rating ****

La Paz
Andalucia 1
Ubeda
Tel: 750848

Modest, unmemorable accommodation in the town.

Open all year
Rooms: 61
Credit cards: Diner's Club, Visa
Rating **

EATING OUT

The finest restaurant in town is that in the parador itself, where the waitresses, unusually for a parador, wear colourful local costumes. The menu covers both local and international dishes. A typical regional meal might begin with marinated partridge salad – preceded by small tapas of spiced meatballs or *albondigas*, a feuillete of roquefort, deep-fried cheese and fish– followed by mountain kid stewed with pine nuts. The list of *postres* is imaginative – such as *natillas*, a light milk pudding served with deep-fried spiced pastries, a dish that betrays its Moorish origins.

The local bars are proud of their tapas which inevitably include the local speciality of *pipirrana*, tomato, cucumber, onion and marinated fish in a dressing with hard boiled eggs. In La Taberna, next to Cusco (see below), the innkeeper patiently broke an egg, fried a little potato and onion, and then served me with a tiny omelette on a piece of bread no more than two inches across... all for the price of a beer. The bar Ventura Lorento, in the Plaza del Primera de Mayo near the parador, serves excellent *pipirrana* and the surprisingly good white wine from the nearby town of Torreperogil.

Cusco
Parque Vandelvira 8
Ubeda
Tel: 753413

Grill restaurant with largely international cuisine.

Closed Sunday night
Credit cards: Eurocard, Visa
Rating ***

Juanito
Paseo Arca del Agua
Tel: 740040
Baeza

Locally respected hotel dining room serving reliable, if predictable, dishes.

Closed Sunday night and the first two weeks of November
Credit cards: Diner's Club, Eurocard, Visa
Rating ***

UBEDA: USEFUL INFORMATION

Tourist office:	Plaza del Ayuntamiento
	Tel: 750897
Population:	28,717

BAEZA

Tourist office:	Plaza del Pópulo
	Tel: 740444
Population:	14,799

Ubeda

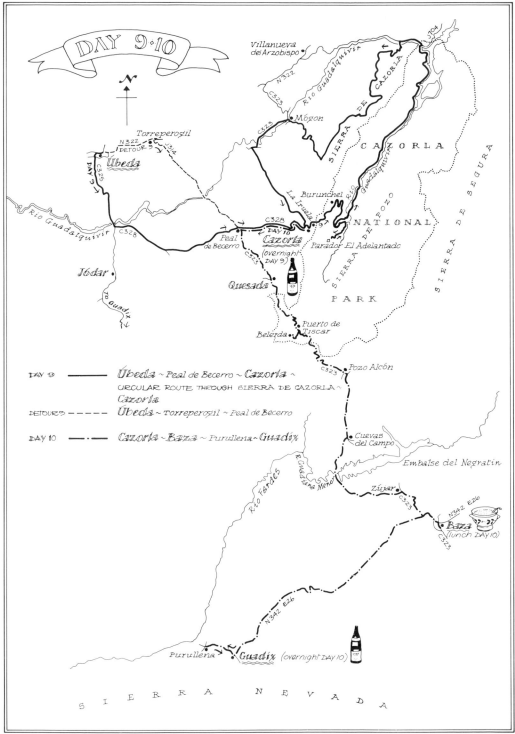

DAY 9·10

N

Villanueva
del Arzobispo

J704

N322

Rio Guadalquivir

SIERRA DE CAZORLA

C323

Mógon

Torreperogil
N322
DETOUR 9
J314

Úbeda
C325

SIERRA DE CAZORLA

CAZORLA

DAY 9

Rio Guadalquivir

C328

Burunchel

La Iruela
J9

SIERRA DE SEGURA

Rio Guadalquivir

SIERRA DE POZO

NATIONAL

C328

Peal
de Becerro

C328

DAY 10

Cazorla
(overnight
DAY 9)

Parador El Adelantado

Jódar

ro Guadix

Quesada

PARK

Belerda

Puerto de
Tíscar

Pozo Alcón
C323

DAY 9 ——— Úbeda ~ Peal de Becerro ~ Cazorla ~
CIRCULAR ROUTE THROUGH SIERRA DE CAZORLA ~
Cazorla

DETOURS - - - - - Úbeda ~ Torreperogil ~ Peal de Becerro

DAY 10 —·—·— Cazorla ~ Baza ~ Purullena ~ Guadix

Cuevas
del Campo

Embalse del Negratin

R. Fardes

R. Guadiana Menor

Zújar
C323

N342 E26

Baza
(lunch DAY 10)
C323

N342 E26

Purullena   Guadix (overnight DAY 10)

S I E R R A   N E V A D A

DAY 9

Ubeda to the Sierra de Cazorla, around 100 miles including a circular tour of the sierra.

Close to Ubeda, the Sierra de Cazorla is one of Spain's ten national parks, a remote region of mountain peaks which is the source of the great Guadalquivir river. The route runs to the mountain town of Cazorla and then into the sierra itself, along the valley of the Guadalquivir, and returning to Cazorla.

Overnight in Cazorla.

Map references
Ubeda	38° 04′N 3° 22′W
Cazorla	37° 55′N 3° 00′W
Burunchel	37° 58′N 2° 58′W

Breakfast at Ubeda.

We are now on the very fringes of Andalucia where the climate is more akin to that of the central plain of Spain – boiling hot in summer, cold in winter – than that of the south. And one can feel this change in spirit in the people themselves; it is a quieter, more conservative region than that of Córdoba, more staid and more pious. In Ubeda's quiet streets and plazas, it seems hard to believe today that this piety and conservatism led to bitter fighting in the town during the Civil War, and recriminations on both sides which led to much church property being damaged or destroyed.

Sierra de Cazorla

From here we turn south into one of Spain's ten national parks, the Sierra de Cazorla, an area of great natural beauty unexpected after the harsh hills of olives which surround Ubeda. There is a fast route by the road to Albacete turning right to follow the signs to Cazorla in Torreperogil, a town remarkable for nothing except the unusually excellent white table wine found in the everyday cafés of the area. A more attractive, but slower way lies to the south. Leave Ubeda by the C325 marked for Jodar, then turn left after crossing the Guadalquivir 14 miles out of Ubeda. The road is marked for Peal de Becerro.

The Cazorla range marks the eastern boundary of the province of Jaen. A dammed section of the Guadalquivir divides it from the Sierra de Segura to the east. In this vast, wild region deer, wild boar and sheep, and the handsome mountain goat, the *Caprica hispanica*, roam under the protection of the national conservation agency ICONA. There are more than 1,300 different kinds of flora in the sierra and an extraordinary range of birds, eagles and hawks are common, the osprey less so, although the skilled birdwatcher, with a guide, may be able to track down a pair in the Cabrilla area. The most amateur observer is bound to catch sight of some colourful creature or plant in the national park, and an excellent information centre has been built in its heart to help visitors make the most of their visit.

Foreign visitors are relatively rare in Cazorla. Most tourists are from Madrid or other large Spanish cities, many of whom come for the expensive and strictly controlled hunting. Facilities are simple and the chances of finding an English-speaking hotelier somewhat rare. The one exception is the parador of Adelantado which is hidden in its own grounds in the depths of the mountains and must count as one of the most secluded hotels in Spain.

Cazorla

The principal town is Cazorla itself, which returns us to familiar Andalucia with its whitewashed houses draped in flowers set on a steep hillside. Three castles stand guard over the area; the lowest, housing a small museum dedicated to mountain life, can be reached by a very poor road or on foot at the back of the town, near the ruins of the Church of Santa Maria. Cazorla is a busy, congested town during the summer. It is best to leave the car outside and walk. The location is certainly spectacular, but it is a modest, unsophisticated place and I would advise the visitor to stay outside, in the sierra, to best appreciate the region.

The road is on the left as you enter Cazorla, badly marked 'Sierra'. Just before leaving the town there is an information office for the national park which has comprehensive leaflets on the flora and fauna of the area. A road to the right leads above Cazorla to the small village close to the jagged ruins of La Iruela castle. It is an attractive little community, less hurried than Cazorla, and the views from the heights are magnificent.

There is an established motoring route through the sierra which begins at Cazorla and loops back to the town. From La Iruela one passes the small village of Burunchel and then enters the national park at a checkpoint where car numbers are taken. This is all part of the security maintained by ICONA; the pursuit of fish and game is strictly controlled within the park, each kill attracts a fixed charge according to the species.

After the checkpoint the road climbs to more than 1400 feet and stands over the unspoilt valley of the Guadalquivir. A turn to the right leads to the remote parador, five miles away, and there is also a much longer expedition to the source of the Guadalquivir. It is an important river to the Spaniard, of course, as significant as the Thames is to the Englishman, but I doubt many foreign visitors would find the lengthy drive worthwhile. Whether one stays at the parador or not, it is a good starting place for walks in the forest.

The main sierra road now descends into the Guadalquivir valley, and you can see the river swelling in size and force as the mountain torrents feed it from both sides. There are a few beds available in local cottages most of the year, a handful of small restaurants and busy campsites. At Torre del Vinagre the Junta de Andalucia has established an excellent information centre which goes some way to explain the complex ecosystem of the region. There is advice on where to look for particular animals in the park which just might help you spot a mountain goat further along the tour.

On the same site there is a botanical garden which, for once, is precisely what it says: a scientific collection of the plants, flowers and trees of Spain displayed according to their type. It is not the Generalife – there is little attempt at aesthetic gardening – but the amateur botanist will find it fascinating.

The road follows the rapidly broadening river and crosses the dam at the edge of the game park. Here there is a right turn into the Sierra de Segura, an area of equal beauty but one which will be beyond the reach of the traveller with only a day to spare. The left turn, marked for Villanueva del Arzobispo, soon branches left and runs through high pine forests to Mogon from where one can return to Cazorla.

Overnight in Cazorla or environs.

ACCOMMODATION

Sierra de Cazorla
La Iruela
Cazorla
Tel: 720015

Quiet, modern hotel with good views in La Iruela, offering far better accommodation than any of the modest establishments in Cazorla itself.

Open all year
Rooms: 60
Facilities: outdoor pool
Credit cards. Diner's Club, Visa
Rating **

Parador El Adelantado
Sierra de Cazorla
Tel: 721075

Modern hotel in secluded forest 15 miles from Cazorla, with beautiful grounds and views. Luxurious accommodation popular with hunters.

Open all year
Rooms: 33
Credit cards: American Express, Diner's Club, Eurocard, Visa
Rating ****

EATING OUT

The parador has a first class dining room which is one of the few restaurants in the area. Local taverns offer standard menus on which *choto* (mountain kid) commonly features, but one should not expect to dine out in style in this rather remote part of Spain. Venison, wild goat, and boar commonly feature on tavern menus and are normally casseroled, served with fried potatoes. There are taverns in Burunchel and Cazorla, and the occasional roadside inn in the valley of the Guadalquivir. Opening hours, menus and quality are erratic.

115

CAZORLA: USEFUL INFORMATION	
Park office:	Martínez Falero 11
	Tel: 720125
Population:	10,005
Facilities:	fishing, hunting, swimming

Guadix

DAY 10

Cazorla to Guadix, around 110 miles.

From Cazorla, the journey follows a little-used mountain route south to emerge on the eroded sandstone plain leading to the town of Guadix, an early home of Spanish Christianity. It is an area where many people continue to live in caves hewn out of the soft rock.

Overnight in Guadix.

Route shown p. 110.

Map references

Cazorla	37° 55´N 3° 00´W
Quesada	37° 50´N 3° 05´W
Cuevas del Campo	37° 35´N 2° 55´W
Baza	37° 30´N 2° 45´W
Guadix	37° 18´N 3° 08´W

Granada

Breakfast in Cazorla.

Our route now heads south for the coast, into a hot and dusty countryside which is more typically Andalucian than that of Ubeda and Cazorla. This is the least frequently visited region, although the next two days include two memorable mountain passes of spectacular beauty. The first takes us from the high ground around Cazorla into the flat agricultural plain which borders the province of Almería.

Leaving Cazorla, the route returns to Peal de Becerro, and then turns left, on the C323, signposted for Pozo Alcón and Baza. In the depths of winter, this road is occasionally closed by snow. In that event there will be a sign as you leave the white, hillside village of Quesada. If you are unlucky enough to find the road blocked – and this is a rare occurence – return to Peal de Becerro and then continue along the route taken from Ubeda, to the C325, travelling south through Jodar to Guadix. After Quesada, the road moves into the Sierra de Pozo, finally reaching the Puerto de Tiscar at 1294 feet. There is a short walk to a tower which offers excellent views.

As we descend, there are extraordinary rock formations formed by erosion and ahead lies the plain which eventually leads to Baza. Soon you come to the Santuario of Tiscar, an old hostel – with even older fortifications above it – which has been built between two rocky outcrops, one of which houses a tunnel for the road. It is an ideal candidate for a new parador and will surely become one as more people begin to learn about this route south from Ubeda. At the moment, one rarely meets a car between Quesada and the plain town of Cuevas del Campo. After the Santuario a side road leads down to the village of Belerda where there is one of the few opportunities for a coffee on this road.

The plain of the valley ahead now takes on more strange forms, the soft stone pitted into bizarre shapes by the centuries. This seems an unlikely area to find a thriving agricultural industry, yet it appears after Pozo Alcón, fed by complex canals and water channels which thread through the fields along the side of the road. The great dam which stops the Guadiana Menor has formed a bright blue lake much larger than that of the Guadalquivir in the Sierra de Cazorla; even hardened lorry drivers stop here to admire the panorama. After Zújar, we meet the busy N342, the principal route from Granada to Murcia along which grain trucks and fish lorries rush as fast as they dare. There is a brief excursion east for those seeking lunch, to the little town of Baza two miles away. A short walk in Baza reveals a different identity. Gone is the dourness of the mountains and one can once again feel the verve and activity of the south. The modest historic monuments of which the town boasts are unlikely to detain the visitor, but there are good restaurants and the atmosphere is engaging.

Lunch in Baza.

Guadix now lies 30 miles to the west, along a fast road lined with truckers' cafés and the occasional craftsman selling home-made pottery, a trade which goes back several centuries. As you leave Baza you will see the first of many cave houses, built into the soft rock, which are the region's most famous feature.

The Baza route is the ideal approach to Guadix since it gives you the best view to be found of this very odd town. Above stands the Sierra Nevada, white-capped as usual, while in the plain sits an enormous red sandstone cathedral, the old cave dwellers' quarter behind it, and all around the humps and contortions of eroded rock outcrops. It is a scene from the imagination of the writers of fantasy fiction.

Purullena

Before settling in the town continue along the main road to Purullena, three miles to the west, where one may look down upon the bizarre valley from a different viewpoint. It is to Purullena that the tourist is guided, for here there is a string of shops and small restaurants catering for the passing trade. Some of the pottery work has charm, and there are more cave dwellings. The life of the modern Spanish troglodyte is by no means frugal. The dwellings usually have electricity and a telephone and you will often find a television aerial attached to the rock roof. There is even a fashion for making some caves overtly luxurious, with the furniture and trappings expected of some modern-day penthouses, though unfortunately you are unlikely to be invited into these fashionable apartments.

The troglodyte life makes a great deal of sense here. The plain is hot and dusty – you may develop a Guadix sore throat in the midst of summer – and the cool dark interiors of the caves offer some escape from the blazing midday temperatures. Nor should it be assumed that all cave dwellers are gypsies – this is simply not the case. The main cave area in Guadix itself is on the hill above the cathedral, and the visitor who looks curious will normally be invited into a private home, for which a tip of 100 pesetas might be appropriate.

Guadix

Modern Guadix is strangely unsophisticated – there are no hotels or restaurants of any note, nor any real attempt to engage the interest of the visitor. The siesta here seems to go on for most of the day. The 16th-century cathedral, in which the familiar Diego Siloé had a hand, is the focal point of the community, and one may park near it with relative ease. There is nothing inside of great interest and, after such a vivid introduction, it seems always surprising that Guadix is not as exotic at close quarters as it appears from a distance. Yet the town has a distinguished history and was an important Roman colony. It may even claim to be the birthplace of Spanish Christianity, through its local martyr Saint Torquatus who is said to have been the first to die for his faith in Roman Iberia. If this is true then the site of the cathedral, itself built on a mosque which replaced a Visigothic church, may be where the country's first Christian place of worship stood. It is all conjecture, of course, and there is little enthusiasm in sleepy Guadix to investigate matters further.

These main sights apart, the town itself has nothing to mark it out from any other small Andalucian community. The Plaza de las Palomas is a fetching galleried square in which drivers are advised to 'mind the doves', though whether this is a sign of an unexpected excitability on the part of the natives or, more likely, drowsiness on the part of the birds themselves is unexplained.

One strange ceremony links Guadix to nearby Baza. Each September 8, an emissary leaves Guadix in order to steal the statue of the Virgin. He is pursued around Baza by screaming inhabitants who have covered themselves in motor oil and – this will come as no surprise – fails to escape with his prize. As I said, this is an unsophisticated region.

Overnight in Guadix.

ACCOMMODATION

Carmen
Ctra. de Granada
Guadix
Tel: 661500

Popular modest hotel on the busy road to Granada.

Open all year
Rooms: 20
Credit cards: Visa
Rating **

Comercio
Mira de Amezcua 3
Guadix
Tel: 660500

Inexpensive hostel accommodation in the town.

Open all year
Rooms: 21
Credit cards: Diner's Club, Eurocard, Visa
Rating **

EATING OUT

Restaurante La Curva
Ctra. de Granada
Baza
Tel: 700002

Excellent fish and grilled meats in a popular local restaurant close to the traffic lights as you enter the town. Easy parking.

Open all year
Credit cards: Visa
Rating ***

One hunts for a memorable restaurant in vain in Guadix. This is small-town, rural Spain with plenty of modest bars serving a wholly acceptable range of tapas and not a single restaurant worthy of mention. My advice is to go native and work your way around the town centre on a tapas crawl. No restaurant in Guadix seemed worthy of the expense, at the time of writing, yet the tapas were as reliable as one would expect. Readers' recommendations will be warmly welcomed.

GUADIX: USEFUL INFORMATION	
Population:	19,860
BAZA	
Population:	20,609

DAY 11

Guadix to the Alpujarra, around 80 miles.

A second spectacular mountain pass travels through the Sierra Nevada into the Alpujarra, a secluded region of picturesque mountain villages which lies behind the western coastline of Andalucia. The Alpujarra is well known in Spain for wind-cured mountain hams, local honey and fruit, and as the home of artists and writers.

Overnight in the Alpujarra.

Route shown on p. 131.

Map references

Guadix	37° 18′N 3° 08′W
La Calahorra	37° 10′N 3° 03′W
Puerto de la Ragua	37° 08′N 3° 01′W
Puerto del Suspiro del Moro	37° 05′N 3° 35′W
Yegen	36° 58′N 3° 05′W
Lanjarón	36° 53′N 3° 30′W
Bubión	36° 55′N 3° 23′W
Trevélez	37° 00′N 3° 15′W
Orgiva	36° 50′N 3° 25′W
Castaras	36° 53′N 3° 15′W

Breakfast in Guadix.

Leave Guadix by the N324 marked for Almería, past more cave homes and along another dusty plain. These sombre landscapes were once popular with film-makers for 'spaghetti westerns' (though 'paella western' might have been more appropriate). Several were shot in the vicinity and at least one used the parador at Ubeda as a ready-made set. There is an odd relic of these days near Tabernas, along the road which leads to Almería, where a western town built for one of the films has been preserved. Locals dress for the part and stage mock fights for passing tourists. Almería, it must be said, is somewhat short of conventional tourist facilities.

La Calahorra

We leave the road before the sound of sixguns, however, turning south towards the castle of La Calahorra which can be seen soon after leaving Guadix. This is an Italianate fortress with a renowned Renaissance patio, the rounded forms of the fortress coming as something of a shock when one has become accustomed to the idea that the castles of southern Spain will normally bear the foursquare characteristics of their Moslem antecedents. To visit the castle you must park in the village and walk up a steep path. This is not an exercise to be recommended in the middle of a summer day, and the rewards are in any case not so great that they should engage the traveller who is short of time.

Just before the village there is a turning marked for the Puerto de la Ragua, a scenic mountain pass which will take us over the Sierra Nevada and into the Alpujarra. This can be blocked by snow in the depths of winter – a sign at La Calahorra indicates whether or not it is open. The alternative routes are substantially longer, and if you are travelling in the middle of winter it may be wise to check the state of the route a few days ahead and plan to go around it if the conditions are difficult. Your hotel will usually be willing to call the authorities to find out about the state of local roads. If Puerto de la Ragua is blocked, the shortest route to the Alpujarra is found by returning to Granada and taking the scenic N323 road to Motril, which passes close to the area. One famous spot on this road is the Puerto del Suspiro del Moro – the Moor's Sigh. It was supposedly here that Boabdil took a last look at the glorious city he had just lost and shed a tear. The view of Granada is certainly memorable, but it is a shame that a modern restaurant has been erected at the top of the hill.

Let us hope that the Puerto de la Ragua is open – as it usually is – for this is a much less travelled route and one which offers a good introduction to the wilder side of the Alpujarra.

Puerto de la Ragua

From La Calahorra the road winds into the sierra through pine forests. Behind lies the dusty vega of Guadix, with the town at its centre. An occasional shepherd or forester might be seen by the side of the road, but otherwise the route is usually uninhabited. The sierra is crossed at Puerto de la Ragua at 2179 feet, then the road runs down the side of a ravine, past gorse and broom to descend into the eastern end of the Alpujarra. Just before Laroles there is a right turn marked for Orgiva and it is this which takes us into the heart of the region.

The Alpujarra

If the English visitor has heard of the Alpujarra at all, it will usually be through the work of the late writer Gerald Brenan who spent most of his life in the village of Yegen which we pass after Mecina Alfahar and Valor. It is one of the area's more modest villages and there are few visible signs to reveal what attracted Brenan, an Englishman of refined tastes, to it. His best known work in English is *South of Granada*, in which he documents the folklore, culture and everyday life of the remote villagers. He is better known in Spain for a series of books on Iberian culture which are standard reference works in a country not short of heavyweight titles about itself.

Brenan was a remarkable man who had a curious end. In his nineties and palpably senile, he was taken back to England to live in an old people's home. This created an enormous uproar in Spain when the newspapers happened upon the story, for every Spaniard was aware that the great Sr Brenan was more Spanish than British – which was undoubtedly true. Money was raised to pay for his return and care in Yegen and the great man died in the Alpujarra that he lovingly recorded over four decades. He is not the only great English writer to live to a rather sad old age in Spain;

Robert Graves had a similar end in Mallorca, though he was spared the trip back to the land of his birth for a stay in an old people's home.

It is tempting to say that the everyday life of the Alpujarra has changed little since *South of Granada,* but this is untrue. The region still adheres to its own customs and feels itself apart from the rest of Andalucia. This is nothing new: it has had a rebellious nature since its natives clashed with the Romans. It was to here that the bedraggled Boabdil and his followers retired after the fall of Granada, and the legacy of Moslem culture led to minor, mildly bloody rebellions with the victorious Christian state for more than a century after 1492.

But the Alpujarra is entering the modern world very quickly. New roads are being built to speed the arrival of the tourist peseta, more hotels and tourist facilities are beginning to appear. The people themselves are markedly less poor than they were a decade ago and, on occasion, have learnt how to slip in the odd illicit item on a restaurant bill.

This does not make the Alpujarra less delightful – but one should be wary of total captivation. The winding roads move through wonderful scenery, the locals are still a little puzzled by the arrival of a foreigner, and there are small surprises around many corners.

It is also a large region which can take several days to explore to the full. The visitor with less time should stick to a set circuit which will provide a good insight into the variety of the area.

The two principal towns are Lanjarón and Orgiva, the latter being about a two-hour drive through the mountains from the turn-off at Laroles. There is good accommodation in Lanjarón and at the small village of Bubión. The best drive is along the circuit which begins at Orgiva and heads north into the mountains and the two villages of Bubión and Capileira. Both are extremely pretty, with the flat-roofed white houses typical of the Alpujarra and dramatic settings on the side of the sierra. The road from Capileira is the same one which we used on the other side of the mountain when visiting the Sierra Nevada from Granada. Even if it is closed, one may drive part of the way and find good viewpoints.

Lunch at Bubión.

From Bubión the road continues east through Pitres and Busquistar and then returns to the mountains to reach Trevélez which claims that at 1614 feet it is the highest village in Europe. Some bright spark in the tourist business has seen fit to label Trevélez the 'Switzerland of the Costa del Sol', attracting the odd, bemused coachload of visitors expecting something rather different. The best mountain hams of the Alpujarra come from here. You can see them being hung in the curing houses and parts of the village smell of *jamón serrano*. Only the *jamón* of Jabugo, in western Andalucia, has a higher reputation. There is trout fishing in the mountain stream at Trevélez, a few basic cafés, and an opportunity for the hearty to climb to the top of the village along mule tracks which pass houses where livestock and humans share the same roof. It is closer to the old Alpujarra than anywhere else on this drive.

The return route runs down the mountain on the far side of the ravine which leads to Trevélez. Take the right turn marked to Castaras at the foot of the ravine to reach a mirador with views back to Trevélez and across to Busquistar. The next sign left is a cul de sac to Castaras, another impressive village set on a rocky outcrop. The church is reminiscent of Granada, and there are the remains of fortifications. The right turn at this junction goes to Orgiva, via Almegijar and Torvizcon. At the former, you will find a short walk to a stone cross marking a mirador. The road rejoins the route we took into Orgiva on our arrival.

Orgiva is more typical of the Alpujarra than Lanjarón, but in neither town is there much to be seen. What pleasures are to be had come from wandering the streets and admiring the selection of fruit and honey on display, and perhaps stopping for a plate of mountain food, *jamón* or *migas*, with a glass of the local deep rosé wine.

Lanjarón is the home of one of Andalucia's most popular mineral waters, and the bottling plant is glass-sided to allow the visitor the chance to see how the mountain springs are captured and then, for *agua mineral con gas*, carbonated.

Overnight in the Alpujarra.

127

ACCOMMODATION

A room can always be found somewhere in the Alpujarra by asking in a bar. Many residents effectively offer bed and breakfast on demand and it would not be risking a great deal to turn up in summer without a booking if one was prepared to accept this kind of simple accommodation.

Villa Turistica de Bubión
Bubión
Tel: 763111/763112/763136

The most comfortable accommodation in the Alpujarra, a new development funded by the state which lies within walking distance of both Bubión and Capileira. Large apartment rooms and excellent views. Highly recommended.

Open all year
Rooms: 43
Credit cards: Diner's Club, Eurocard, Visa
Rating ***

Mesón Poqueira
Dr. Castilla 8
Capileira
Tel: 763048

Simple village rooms and restaurant serving local dishes.

Open all year
Rooms: 17
No credit cards
Rating **

Miramar
Av. Generalissimo 10
Lanjarón
Tel: 770161

Standard, middle-range hotel popular with Spanish visitors.

Open all year
Rooms: 60
Facilities: outdoor pool
Credit cards: American Express, Diner's Club, Eurocard, Visa
Rating ***

Paraiso
Av. Generalissimo 18
Lanjarón
Tel: 770012

Close to the Miramar with much the same kind of ambience.

Open all year
Rooms: 49
Credit cards: American Express, Diner's Club, Eurocard, Visa
Rating **

EATING OUT

One should eat the wonderful ham, washed down with a glass of local wine, *migas* – breadcrumbs fried with peppers and garlic – *choto*, and the excellent local fruit. *Patatas a lo Pobre* – poor man's potatoes – are a common tapas, fried in olive oil with garlic and peppers. Honey from the sierra is exceptionally cheap and good. Restaurant menus vary little from establishment to establishment, and opening hours are distinctly erratic. It would be a good idea to check with your accommodation on what restaurants are open during your visit.

Granada

Taberna El Secadero
Bubión
Tel: 763130

Small tavern specialising in *jamón*, cheese and local wines, close to the Villa Turistica. Reached by a private lane leading off the main road from Bubión to Capileira.

Open all year
No credit cards
Rating **

Teide
Bubión
Tel: 763037

Local dishes in an atmospheric house.

Open all year
No credit cards
Rating **

In Capileira there are several interesting small bars serving tapas. La Chimenea is in a typical flat-roofed house overlooking the mountains as you enter the village. The Paco Lopez sells several kinds of local sausage, the common *Plato Alpujarreno*, which consists of meat, sausage, eggs and beans, and roast rabbit. Similar small bars in Trevélez, Lanjarón and Orgiva are equally rewarding.

BUBION: USEFUL INFORMATION
Population: 377
ORGIVA
Population: 4,859
LANJARON
Population: 4,094

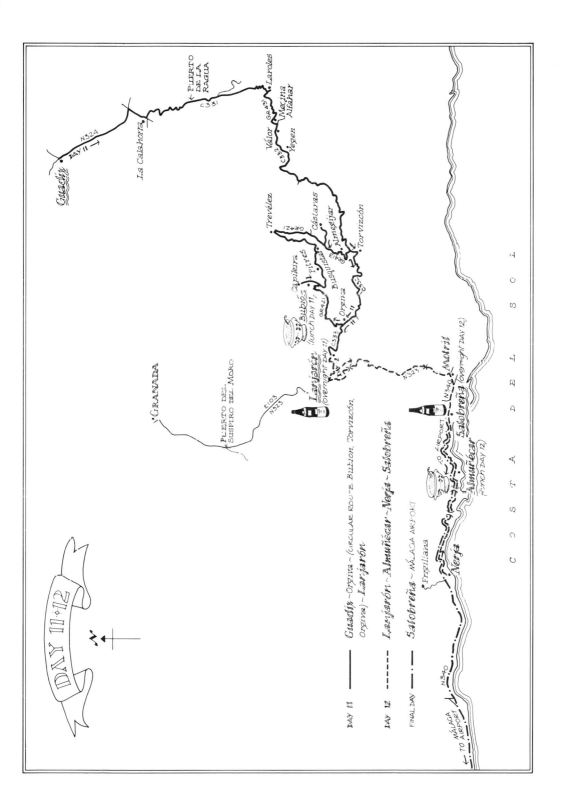

DAY 11·12

DAY 11 ———— Guadix ~ Orgiva ~ (Circular route Bubión, Torvizcón,
Orgiva) ~ Lanjarón

DAY 12 - - - - Lanjarón ~ Almuñécar ~ Nerja ~ Salobreña

FINAL DAY —·—·— Salobreña ~ Málaga airport

GUADIX
N324
DAY 11 →
La Calahorra
← PUERTO
DE LA
RAGUA
C331
Válor
C332
Mecina
Laroles
Alfahar
Yegen
Trevélez
GR421
Cástaras
Almejíjar
Torvizcón
Bubión
Capileira
Pitres
BUSQUISTAR
Orgiva
GR421
C333
Lanjarón
(lunch DAY 11)
(overnight DAY 11)
N1
GRANADA
PUERTO DEL
SUSPIRO DEL MORO
PUERTO DEL
MORO
E103
N323
N323
Motril
N340
Salobreña
(overnight DAY 12)
TO AIRPORT
Almuñécar
(lunch DAY 12)
Frigiliana
Nerja
N340
MÁLAGA
AIRPORT
← TO MÁLAGA
AIRPORT
MÁLAGA AIRPORT

C O S T A   D E L   S O L

DAY 12

From the Alpujarra to the Mediterranean coast, around 70 miles from Capileira to Nerja.

The coast east of Málaga is less developed than the Costa del Sol. There are several quiet places by the sea, a popular parador, and an excellent range of restaurants. Accommodation is available in three very different seaside towns, Salobreña, Almuñécar and Nerja.

Overnight in Salobreña, Almuñécar or Nerja.

Route shown p. 131.

Map references
Salobreña	36° 45´N 3° 38´W
Almuñécar	36° 44´N 3° 42´W
Nerja	36° 47´N 3° 51´W

Breakfast in the Alpujarra.

Like Circe's island, the Alpujarra, with its mountain air and unhurried atmosphere, does not encourage the visitor to move on. Yet less than two hours away lies the stretch of Mediterranean coastline which runs east of Málaga to Almería, where there are still parts which are relatively untouched by the massive tourist development seen elsewhere on the Costa del Sol.

I would always end a tour of Andalucia in a quiet hotel by the coast. After the round of cities and mountains, there is something infinitely relaxing about being able to walk within earshot of the sea and to smell the salt air, with little in the way of sights to tick off. This stretch of coastline remains scenic. There are old watchtowers on remote headlands, sudden *corniches* on the road as it sweeps by the sea, and the occasional interruption of traffic by a herd of sleek goats being led by a farmer who is oblivious to the changing face of the Andalucian coast. One cannot pretend that the area is untouched by tourism. Giant villa developments are creeping across the hillsides all along the coast. But this also has one welcome side effect. After almost a fortnight of eating Spanish food, the palate of even the greatest admirer of Andalucian cuisine can become jaded. In this part of the coast, the presence of foreign residents has brought about an influx of fine restaurants representing a range of European cookery styles.

Salobreña

To leave the Alpujarra join the main Granada-Motril road, the N323, which winds through the mountains down to the coast. If you have not had time to see Lanjarón, now is the opportunity, since one spur of the route from the Alpujarra goes through the town. As the drive approaches sea level, you are surrounded by fields full of abundant crops, one of the most popular being sugar cane. In the distance, to the right, Salobreña appears, marked by fortifications overlooking the sea.

Turn right on reaching the N340 – Motril is an industrial port of no interest whatsoever – and there is a sudden sweetness in the air. It comes from the factories which mar this view of Salobreña (which looks much more spectacular when approached from the west). These are sugar cane refineries, and next to them, characterised by another significant, sweet smell, is the rum refinery of *Bermudez Ron*. Here visitors can see the process of turning the by-products of sugar refining into a powerful rum – a spirit which has been produced in this part of Spain for a good two centuries.

Salobreña is a photogenic town. Old white houses cling to the rocky hill lining the narrow streets which lead to the old castle. From the ramparts one can, year-by-year, chart the steady growth of property development along a stretch of coastline which was virtually unknown a decade ago. The castle, as you would expect, is an Arab fortification, now rather bare. If this were west of Málaga one would find coach parties, bars and flamenco displays along the walls. Salobreña's offering is a rather dog-eared lion, caged in the keep, who stares, puzzled, at the occasional visitor... but he might have been replaced by something more 'sophisticated' by the time you arrive. Salobreña is a sleepy place, in spite of the rash of hotel building which has claimed the strip of land between the hill and the sea. There is a handful of still authentic bars in the quiet streets where an interesting tapa is offered for nothing, and, out of town, a good, quiet hotel on its own headland.

Almuñécar

Travelling west, after ten miles, lies the small fishing town of Almuñécar which, though growing yearly, remains my favourite stopping place east of Málaga. At heart, this is still a seafaring community, and the tourist industry such as it is remains firmly geared for the domestic market. The town is a historic one; the Carthaginians called it Sexi, a name fondly recalled by the occasional hotel and bar today. In 755 the Moslem leader Abderrahman landed here and was welcomed by the local Arabs. This event led to the foundation of Córdoba as the capital of an independent Moslem state and it was, of course, Abderrahman who began the first section of the Mezquita in Córdoba, with its varied collections of columns and capitals culled from whatever his architects could lay their hands on.

Modern Almuñécar manages to hide its antecedents well. From the road it appears an unexciting town of low villas, but there is more. From the pleasant Parque del Majuelo, which contains the remains of Roman buildings and fish salting pits, you may walk up into the old town, along the original walls and past the ruins of a small castle. Narrow streets run down to the sea to the east and lead to a small fleet of still-active fishing boats. A modest museum, in the Cueva de Siete Palacios, has a collection of Roman and Moslem artefacts.

The two pebbly beaches of the town converge at the Peñon del Santo, a headland with a cross, illuminated at night to send out its benedictions to the seafarer. From here there is a pleasant modern promenade which runs east. In the evening, when the waves crash onto the rocks and salt spray dampens the air, it is the place for the locals to promenade, couples of all ages arm-in-arm. There is a small monument to the English writer Laurie Lee who lived locally for a few years.

Tourists and fish apart, Almuñécar also makes its living from the avocado, one of many imported exotic fruit and vegetables grown from here to Almería as part of the resurgence of Spanish agriculture. Only a few years ago, the prices of avocadoes across the world were posted outside the town hall each day, and one could watch farmers nervously charting movements in New York and Paris just like London brokers monitoring the dollar. The blackboards and pieces of chalk have now gone, along with the sweet avocado dessert which one enthusiastic restaurateur placed on his menu in an outburst of local pride.

A walk along the coast west of the Peñon del Santo takes one to the bay of Cotobro where the villa developments are as unobtrusive as any you will find on this coastline. It is also worth driving this way – leave Almuñécar by the road to Málaga then turn left into the Cotobro development, and right immediately past the restaurant La Courva into Bajada del Mar. A few curves later and there is the chance to park close to a footpath leading to a deserted headland, one of those rare parts of the coast which has been set apart for nature conservation. Swifts, hoopoes and gulls compete for air space and there is an interesting range of Mediterranean coastal flora.

Lunch in Almuñécar or Nerja.

Nerja

Almuñécar is a town that looks to the Alpujarra, as one can see in the products sold in the street market every Friday. The next town along the coast stands in the shadow of Málaga, and is therefore more sophisticated and predictable. Nerja, as one is constantly reminded throughout the town, is known as the 'Balcony of Europe', a name given it in 1885 by the visiting Alfonso XII. Kings are allowed to make such sweeping judgements, of course. The truth is that the view from the Balcón itself, a terrace on the low cliff at the edge of the town, is excellent but no better than may be had from several other points on the coast. Nor, of course, can one see anything of Europe but Spain.

In the 1970s, Nerja became a fashionable place to live for wealthy expatriates who now form an active and sociable community of their own. The building boom began in the early 1980s with the well-known El Capistrano complex. On a hillside on the eastern edge of the town, this was designed to reflect the architecture and community spirit of a true Spanish village which, to an extent, it does, even down to the parking problems. Nerja is growing too fast for its own good, but there is an excellent parador, with a lift to a good beach.

The Cuevas de Nerja, two miles to the east on the main road, are a complex of caves which have long been a great tourist attraction. There are traces of the presence of paleolithic man, including some paintings, and a complex of chambers in which stalagmite and stalactite formations fight for your attention. As a theatrical event, the caves are well done, professionally lit and administered with competence. But the place is often overcrowded and will not appeal to anyone with a trace of claustrophobia.

Just west of Nerja, the village of Frigiliana lies four miles away in the foothills of the Sierra de Tejeda. This is another 'typical village', but Nerja's resistance to the package holiday trade means that it is by no means as tacky as Mijas has become. Some of the low white houses are reminiscent of the Alpujarra, there are views of the coast, and a number of promising restaurants are beginning to open (though none so long-lived that I shall mention them here; the catering trade hereabouts does not have a reputation for longevity).

Wherever one stays on the coast, it is an easy drive back along the coast to Málaga and the more familiar sights of the Costa del Sol where this journey into eastern Andalucia began.

Overnight on the coast (Salobreña, Almuñécar, Nerja).

Granada

ACCOMMODATION

There is a shortage of hotel rooms in all three towns mentioned here, since most visitors to the area stay in villas or self-catering apartments. Advance bookings are essential throughout the year, and it is wise to book several days in advance if you wish to stay at Nerja's popular Parador.

Salobreña
N340 4km
Salobreña
Tel: 610286

On its own headland east of the town, the Salobreña has good views, reasonable rooms, and absolute quiet. Unfinished building on the headland mars the view.

Open all year
Rooms: 80
Facilities: tennis, terraces and outdoor pool
Credit cards: American Express, Diner's Club, Eurocard, Visa
Rating ***

Tropical
Av. de Europa 8
Almuñécar
Tel: 633458

Inexpensive, friendly small hotel with comfortable modern rooms close to the beach.

Open all year
Rooms: 11
Credit cards: Visa
Rating **

Goya
Av. General Galindo
Almuñécar
Tel: 630550

Close to the Tropical and similar, except that it has a dining room and a loyal business clientele.

Open all year
Rooms: 24
Credit cards: Visa
Rating **

Parador de Nerja
Playa de Burriana
Nerja
Tel: 520050

Luxurious modern parador to the east of town, with a private lift to a first class beach. Booking is essential. The restaurant is bland and predictable, best avoided for dinner.

Open all year
Rooms: 60
Facilities: lift to beach, tennis, outdoor pool
Credit cards: American Express, Diner's Club, Eurocard, Visa
Rating ****

Balcón de Europa
Paseo Balcón de Europa 1
Nerja
Tel: 520800

Situated on the famous terrace, the hotel has good views and little else to commend it. Fine if you can stand being in the midst of the tourist bustle.

Rooms: 105
Credit cards: Diner's Club, Eurocard, Visa
Rating ***

Granada

Al Andalus
Urb. Ladera del Aguila
Nerja
Tel: 521022

Small hotel with views near the caves two miles out of town.

Open all year
Rooms: 12
No credit cards
Rating ***

EATING OUT

La Courva
Bajada del Mar (no telephone)
Almuñécar

Just after the first turnoff to Cotobro from Almuñécar, this is a Belgian-run restaurant featuring French specialities. There is a small terrace with views over the bay. Specialities include goat's cheese with artichoke, duck with wild mushrooms, swordfish in champagne sauce, and steak with a selection of different sauces.

Open all year
Credit cards: American Express, Diner's Club, Eurocard, Visa
Rating ***

Los Geranios
Pl. de la Rosa 4
Almuñécar
Tel: 630724

Very popular restaurant with outside tables in square at the foot of the old town. The decor is attractively Andalucian and the menu international: sole dishes and fondue are among the specialities. Booking advisable.

Closed Wednesdays and November 10 to December 10
Credit cards: American Express, Diner's Club, Eurocard, Visa
Rating ***

Amadeus
Av. de Europa, Parque El Majuelo
Almuñécar
Tel: 632855

Austrian specialities in stylish, modern restaurant opposite the park.

Closed Wednesdays
Credit cards: American Express, Diner's Club, Eurocard, Visa
Rating ***

Pepe Rico
Almirante Ferrándiz 31
Nerja
Tel: 520247

Excellent international cuisine which attracts customers from miles around
– booking essential. Specialities include scampi Café de Paris.

Closed Thursdays and December
Credit cards: American Express, Diner's Club, Eurocard, Visa
Rating ****

ALMUNECAR: USEFUL INFORMATION

Tourist office:	Puerta del Mar
	Tel: 631125
Population:	16,141
Facilities:	beaches, coastal walks

NERJA

Tourist office:	Puerta del Mar
	Tel: 521531
Population:	12,012
Facilities:	beaches, golf

SALOBRENA

Population:	8,119
Facilities:	beaches, golf

Cazorla

Recipes
from the Region

MENU 1

Ajo blanco
Cold almond, grape and garlic soup

. . .

Choto ajillo
Kid (or lamb) in garlic casserole

. . .

Natillas con torrijas
Spiced custard with bread fingers

Ajo blanco
Cold almond, grape and garlic soup

4 oz/125g almonds
2 cloves garlic
3 slices dry white bread,
crusts removed
1/4 pt/150 ml olive oil
3 tbsp wine vinegar
2 pts/1.2l water
1lb/500g green grapes
salt to taste

Serves 4/6

This unusual cold soup is one of the many variations of gazpacho found in Andalucia. It is served beautifully by Córdoba's famous *El Caballo Rojo* restaurant, and rarely disappoints. The several conflicting sweet and savoury flavours are difficult to pinpoint for the uninitiated, and the diner could be forgiven for thinking that the soup is a difficult and delicate dish to prepare at home. Nothing could be further from the truth, however. *Ajo blanco* is simple to make, from everyday ingredients, and is a memorable first course for any Spanish meal, particularly on a hot day.

Remove the skin from the almonds by pouring boiling water on them, leaving for a few minutes then rubbing between the fingers. Grind in a food processor or blender with the salt and garlic. Soak the bread in water then squeeze tightly

With the food processor running, gradually add the bread to the almond mixture, then follow with the oil and vinegar. Make the mixture fluid with a little of the water, then transfer to a large serving bowl, add the remaining water and stir well. Add more salt or vinegar if necessary, then the grapes, seeded and preferably peeled. Chill well and stir before serving.

Warning: garlic cloves can vary greatly in strength from purchase to purchase. Before using a head of garlic blind in this recipe, it is worthwhile trying the cloves in another dish to ascertain whether you have a particularly fiery bulb. If you have, then reduce the amount of garlic accordingly.

145

Choto ajillo
Kid in garlic casserole

2 lb/1kg kid or stewing
lamb
1 slice bread
3 cloves garlic
1/2 bottle white wine
pinch each paprika,
oregano
2 bay leaves
1 tbsp vinegar
salt and pepper
olive oil for frying

Serves 4

Mountain kid, while readily available in some
local Andalucian butchers, is hard to find elsewhere. So make this hearty Andalucian casserole
with lean lamb for an authentic taste of the rich
mountain cuisine.

Brown the chopped garlic and bread in oil and
remove to a casserole. Then brown the diced
meat in the same frying pan. Blend the remaining
herbs with salt, vinegar, and a generous helping of
pepper. Add the meat to the casserole, followed
by the herbs and bay leaves. Cover with wine and
cook in a medium oven for an hour and a half.
Remove bay leaves before serving, and provide
plenty of warm bread for mopping up the juices.

Natillas con torrijas
Spiced custard with bread fingers

1 pt/600ml milk
cinnamon stick
lemon peel
4 egg yolks
3 oz/75g sugar
3 slices dry bread
medium sherry
1 beaten egg

Serves 4

Briefly boil the milk with the cinnamon and
lemon peel then remove from the heat. Beat the
egg yolks and sugar well in a double boiler, then
gradually introduce the milk, stirring constantly.
When the mixture thickens, pour into individual
serving dishes and allow to cool.

Remove the crust from the bread and cut into
finger slices. Dip into sherry then into the beaten
egg and fry in oil or butter until brown. Coat with
cinnamon and sugar, drain and serve cold with
the dessert.

MENU 2

Sopa de ajo
Hot garlic soup

· · ·

Huevos, jamón, chorizo y migas
Eggs, with ham, sausage and breadcrumbs

· · ·

Peras al horno
Pears baked with wine

Sopa de ajo
Hot garlic soup

6 cloves garlic
4 slices bread
4 eggs
2 pt/1.2l water
4 fl. oz/125ml olive oil
salt and pepper

Serves 4

Fry the chopped garlic and bread in the oil in a large pan or, preferably, in a pressure cooker. When golden, stir in water, salt and pepper and simmer, for 20 minutes in a pan or five minutes under pressure. Season to taste and pour soup into heatproof serving dishes. Break an egg into each and poach in a medium oven for a few minutes until set.

147

Huevos, jamón, chorizo y migas
Eggs, with ham, sausage and breadcrumbs

half a dry white loaf
1 clove garlic
1 small onion
4 eggs
1 lb/500g chorizo
(seasoned uncooked
sausage)
4 oz/125g jamón
serrano (raw mountain
ham, like Parma)
paprika
oil

Serves 4

This is a common working class lunch throughout Andalucia, and may be varied by the addition of grilled green peppers. First, prepare the *migas*. Tear the bread into small pieces and dampen lightly. Leave for several hours or overnight. Sauté the finely chopped onion and garlic in a large frying pan until golden, then add the bread. Slowly fry the pieces until they are toasted, adding a little paprika or cumin to colour the dish. The *migas* can be kept warm under a grill while the rest of the meal is prepared.

Cook the sausages and keep warm before preparing, as a last step, the eggs. The Spanish have set ideas about how eggs should be fried. Butter is frowned upon; for a true Spanish egg, the medium must be olive oil deep enough to cover the whole of the egg. Heat the oil to near smoking, break the egg on a saucer then slide it into the pan. The edges should be brown and crinkly, the yolk still runny. Fry each egg individually and serve on a bed of *migas* with the sausage and a slice of ham.

Peras al horno
Pears baked with wine

1 lb/500g pears
3 oz/75g almonds
lemon juice
a quarter bottle of
sweet Malaga wine or
red wine
cinnamon stick
2 cloves

Serves 4

Skin the almonds (see p.145) then peel, core and halve the pears. Sprinkle with a little lemon juice to prevent discoloration, add wine, almonds and spices and bake in a medium oven for around half an hour. Serve with cream.

MENU 3

Pipirrana
Andalucian salad

. . .

Cazón en Adobo
Marinated dogfish

. . .

Higos a la Malagueña
Figs, Malaga Style

Pipirrana
Andalucian salad

2 hard boiled eggs
4 beef tomatoes
2 green peppers
1/2 onion
small tin tuna
2oz/50g ham
1/2 clove garlic
olive oil and wine
vinegar to taste
salt and pepper

Serves 4

A dish of *pipirrana* may be found on the counter of tapas bars throughout the region. Freshly made, it is an excellent salad *entremése.*

Chop the egg whites and set aside the yolks. Chop the tomatoes, onion and peppers, and mix in a salad bowl with the flaked tuna and diced ham. Prawns and other cooked shellfish may be added to the salad to make the common dish of *Salpicon de Mariscos.* Good olives, drained, also make a worthwhile addition.

Mix the yolks with the minced garlic and slowly beat in olive oil followed by vinegar in the proportion of three parts oil to one part vinegar. Pour the dressing over the salad immediately before serving, and accompany with bread to mop up the juices.

Cazón en Adobo
Marinated dogfish

2 lb/1kg dogfish or
other firm fish
1/2pt/300ml each oil
and vinegar
3 cloves garlic
generous pinch each
paprika, cumin and
oregano
flour and oil for frying

Serves 4

The excellent seafood bars of Málaga adore this dish using either gilthead, *dorada,* or dogfish, *cazón,* in other parts of the region.

Any firm fish may be used. It is essential to use good olive oil, heated close to smoking, for perfect results.

The day before, cut the fish into bite-sized slices and remove skin and bone. Chop the garlic and combine all of the ingredients except the flour and oil for frying. Add the fish slices, stir well and leave to marinate overnight in a refrigerator, covered with a plate or film.

Drain the fish well then heat the oil in a deep pan. Dredge the slices in the flour and fry for a few minutes until crisp and golden before serving immediately. The dish may be served with vegetables or alongside the *pipirrana* for an authentic, easy-going tapas meal.

Higos a la Malagueña
Figs, Málaga Style

8 fresh figs
$1/2$ lemon
6 fl. oz/175ml Malaga wine or sweet sherry
2 tsp sugar

Serves 4

Wash the figs and, if the skins are tough, peel them. Slice the fruit and place in a bowl with the wine and sugar.

Squeeze the lemon over the mixture and chill for at least two hours before serving, with cream if required.

Glossary of Food Terms

Starters (Entreméses)

arroz brut	dry soup of rice and various meats
arroz marinera	light, saffron and rice soup
boquerones	anchovies, usually in vinegar
croquetas	plain, breadcrumbed chicken croquettes
ensalada de pimientos asados	roast pepper salad
entreméses variados	variety of cooked meats and salads
esparragos	asparagus
flamenquines	ham and cheese rolls, fried
gazpacho	cold soup of tomatoes, peppers, garlic and onion
mejillónes marinara	mussels in strong tomato stock
salpicon de mariscos	seafood cocktail
sopa de ajo	garlic soup
sopa de almendras	filling, hot almond soup
sopa de tomate	local, garlic-flavoured tomato soup

Meats (Carne)

bistec	beefsteak
buey	ox
butifarra	spiced pork sausage
cabrito	kid
carnero	mutton
cerdo	pork
chorizo	highly spiced pork sausage
choto	mountain kid
cordero	lamb
frito	fried offal and vegetables
jamón	ham
pincho	seasoned kebab
sesos	brains
solomillo	sirloin steak
ternera	veal, beef

Poultry and Game (Ave y Caza)

codorniz	quail
conejo	rabbit

jabilí	wild boar
liebre	hare
pato	duck
pavo	turkey
perdiz	partridge
pintada	guinea fowl
pollo	chicken
tordo	thrush
venado	venison

Fish (Pescado)

anchoa	anchovy
anguila	eel
atún	tuna
bacalao	salt cod
besugo	sea bream
cazón	dogfish
chanquete	whitebait
dorada	gilthead
emperador (pez espada)	swordfish
lenguado	sole
lubina	sea bass
merluza	hake
parrillada	grilled selection of fish
rape	monkfish
rodaballo	turbot
salmonete	red mullet
salmón	salmon
sardina	sardine
trucha	trout

Seafood (Mariscos)

almeja	clam
berberecho	cockle
buey de mar	northern crab
calamar	squid
camarón	shrimp
cangrejo	crab

153

centolla	spider crab
chipirón	small squid
choco	large squid, normally from Cádiz
concha fina	Venus clam
cigala	large variety of prawn
gamba	prawn
langosta	lobster
langostino	Dublin Bay prawn
mejillón	mussel
ostra	oyster
percebe	barnacle
pulpo	octopus
sepia	cuttlefish

Vegetables (Verduras)

aguacete	avocado
ajo	garlic
alcachofa	artichoke
alcaparra	caper
berenjena	aubergine
cebolla	onion
champiñones	mushrooms
coliflor	cauliflower
endivas	endives
espárragos	asparagus
garbanzos	chick peas
guisantes	peas
habas	dried broad beans
judías	green beans
lechuga	lettuce
lombarda	red cabbage
patatas	potatoes
pepinillo	cucumber
pimiento	pepper
remolacha	beetroot
seta	wild mushroom
tomate	tomato
verdura	greens
zanahoria	carrot

Fruit (Fruta)

albaricoque	apricot
cereza	cherry
ciruela	plum
clementina	mandarin orange
fresa	strawberry
granada	pomegranate
higo	fig
lima	lime
limón	lemon
manzana	apple
melocotón	peach
melón	melon
membrillo	quince
naranja	orange
pera	pear
plátano	banana
uva	grape

Selected Bibliography

South from Granada, Gerald Brenan, Cambridge University Press, 1981. Brenan's best-known work in English documents life in the Alpujarra in the 1930s.

The Foods and Wines of Spain, Penelope Casas, Penguin, 1985. Weighty and comprehensive handbook of traditional recipes and wine lore written by the American wife of an expatriate Spaniard.

LookOut, LookOut Publications, Puebla Lucia, 29640 Fuengirola (Málaga), Spain. Published monthly, *LookOut* is a superb English language magazine guide to the many facets of modern Spain, from life in the resorts to out-of-the-way places to visit. Useful restaurant reviews with an emphasis on the Costa del Sol. Essential for any regular visitor to Spain.

Iberia, James Michener, Random House, 1968. As one would expect of Michener, this vast and highly readable panorama attempts to cover every aspect of the Spanish character and nation... and almost succeeds. Somewhat dated, but widely available in paperback.

Spain, Jan Morris, Penguin, 1982. Well-travelled foreign correspondent turns her attention to the character and culture of modern Spain.

Cooking in Spain, Janet Mendel Searl, LookOut Publications, Spain, 1987. Unquestionably the best English language guide to Spanish cooking currently available. In addition to hundreds of recipes, the author translates virtually every possible ingredient of Spanish dishes and offers advice on selecting wines and buying everyday food in local markets. Invaluable and, at 400 pages for under £5, excellent value.

La Iruela Castle

Geographical Index

Recipes Index